This book is dedicated to my feisty grandmother Nancy, the matriarch of our family. The woman who loved to cook and instilled the value of a homemade meal. Who never showed favoritism to any of her grandchildren, yet made us believe we were each her chosen one. Who created memories in the kitchen that have lasted a lifetime and have been passed down to the next generation. The woman who always encouraged me to believe I could do and be anything and never doubted I wouldn't. Whose handwritten notes and scribbles from her recipes are my most prized possession today. I'm certain she's baking banana bread in heaven.

Shavon Davis Photography

contents

condiments

beverages

sweet treats

introduction

When you come from an Italian family, learning to cook and bake starts at an early age. My happiest childhood memories have always been in the kitchen with my family, watching my mom and grandma. Cooking and baking for every holiday and every birthday was a family affair. If you had two able hands, you were involved in some way in the kitchen. With a pinch on the cheek, you were handed an apron and delegated a task. No one was exempt from helping, nor did anyone want to be.

The love for food has always been there. As soon as I could kneel on a stool by my grandmother at her flour covered butcher-block table and make gnocchi and banana bread, I was hooked. Our passion for cooking and eating has always been our vehicle for showing our love for each other. If you didn't want it, you were still made to try it, at least once. It caused me to expand my childhood palette and become adventurous in the kitchen.

Taking these traditional and beloved recipes of my family and creating a healthier version is a challenge, but one I've grown to love. I am a foodie and I don't deny that. I'm also a health conscious momma who had to give up sugar, but who still wants chocolate.

My love affair with sugar began early on. Not because my mother deprived me of sugar and not because I was brought up in an unhappy or sheltered life. It has always been a joy to eat, a joy to cook and share meals together, but unfortunately for me, sugar became an uncontrollable addiction.

For whatever reason that began in my childhood, sugar became my best friend. I was drawn to the comfort of baked products full of sugar. I was never an obese child. But by high school and throughout college years the sugar addiction became worse, in how I dealt with life, stress, school, grades, work, and relationships.

I can't say why I turned to sugar in my youngest years. I just remember being 15 and thinking I was chubby, so I went on a diet for the first time in my life. I looked through a fad diet book and tried cabbage and onions for a week—yes, a whole week! Then the next week I tried peanut butter and bananas, and it continued on and on, all the while doing a number on my digestion. But then everyone knows what happens with fad diets; they get less appealing as the time goes on, and that's why there's a fad. I did lose weight, but I also learned another way to eat what I wanted and not gain anything. I purged. I found it exciting to be able to have my "cake" and not gain weight. I was bulimic. Before I even realized it, time went on and it grew increasingly harder to hide this secret. I lost my hair, had popped blood vessels around my eyes, and even lost my period for a year. When I began having unexplained sharp pains in my throat I was not sure how much longer I could continue to do this. At the age of 16, I was lost, confused, and depressed, but my obsession to achieve a slim figure was my only focus.

When my parents discovered this situation they immediately sought help for me, and by the grace of God, I recovered. I gained weight and continued to gain, but I lost the desire to purge and have never desired to do so again. I have never shared this information on my blog, so it will be a surprise for many of my fans reading this. But sharing my story in my cookbook now felt right and natural, so here we are.

Although I stopped purging, compulsiveness with sugar continued to torment me. I packed on 30 pounds by the time I graduated high school. I felt drained, exhausted, and unable to break free. College brought new life challenges, but since my focus had changed, and I didn't care that I had extra weight on, sugar helped me deal with those challenges. The vending machine each morning was my fix. Like someone addicted to cigarettes, I needed sugar to start my day. My drug of choice was always the worst sugary item I could find, often a gigantic cinnamon bun.

One year after graduation, at the age of 22, I finally learned I needed support and accountability. Weight Watchers was wonderful and helped me lose weight and maintain my weight for the next 7 years, leading a noncompulsive way of life. By

25 I was married and by 29 I had my first child. Having a baby brought so much joy, but it triggered the obsession with losing the weight gained from pregnancy. I went back to Weight Watchers when my boy turned one, and I thankfully lost the weight and managed well until my second child was born 3 years later. The sugar addiction surfaced again, and I could not lose the weight from having my daughter, nor did Weight Watchers help me this time around. I ate all my points in sugary foods. I was stuck and miserable and desperate.

Through a friend I found a Christian program called Prism that was hard core. To me, anyway. It eliminated white flour and white sugar for 6 weeks—6 weeks! I had never ever done anything like that before and for this sugar addict, it was my worst nightmare. But I needed the accountability, and it worked for me. It stopped becoming just about losing the weight I wanted and more about removing the obsession with sugar and finding freedom. For the next 3 years, I engulfed myself in learning everything I could about making recipes without sugar and refined flours. This became my new obsession, writing recipes, teaching classes at my church, and finding such joy in helping my friends by sharing my recipes. The passion for cooking I'd had as a child was always there, and now it was being transformed into a new exciting challenge to remake healthier recipes of what I loved. I believe God turned what was meant for my destruction into His calling for my life. And I was happy.

In 2004, I was doing everything I loved. I had two children and I was home raising them and tutoring part time. There was no more obsession and my new passion was sustaining me as I continued to abstain from sugar and to help my friends. When I became pregnant with my third child, I was ecstatic, because we had been trying for almost 6 months. Maybe it was hormones from pregnancy or maybe it was pride. I had this whole sugar thing down, or so I thought. I knew what to do to lose weight and I knew how to maintain it. I wrote amazing recipes and helped my friends. I was on top of the world . . . with pride in myself. One day I just decided I could have a little bite of a sugary treat that everyone else was having. *For goodness sake*, I thought. *I'm eating for two again, aren't I? What's the big deal? I've got this*. And I was deceived. Just as Eve was deceived in the garden, I was deceived into believing I could go back to sugar without a problem. I threw all my knowledge out the window. I went back to sugar in that one bite. It was all over for me. The freedom from obsession, the freedom from the pull of sugar, the freedom from cravings escaped me in one mouthful. My justification was that after I had the baby I would just do what I did before to be sugar-free. No problem. Oh how wrong I was! Like a ravenous lion, the pull for sugar was even worse than ever before, harder than I ever imagined it would be. I knew I needed accountability: someone to call, to help to keep me on track, to pray for me. I went back to the Prism program to detox again. This was in 2006, and it was at this point I *finally* realized sugar is my addiction just as much as a drug addict or an alcoholic. I prayed to God that if I could get back the self-control and discipline I had before I had my third child, I would never go back to sugar again. I prayed and He answered. And I have never looked back.

It has been 8 years since then and I'm healthier and happier than I've ever been. I no longer crave sugary treats. No food tempts me where I feel the need to give in to even one bite. I've been there and done that and this way is better. I am truly free. As long as I abstain from sugar and watch how often I consume even natural sugars, I am able to tame that ravenous lion. I am able to keep myself at a normal weight, but more importantly, I am free from cravings.

I wish I could say it was easy, but cutting sugar from my life was anything but. There is no secret pill to take that will remove sugar cravings. It is hard work, but it can be done. I pray daily to God for strength to abstain, one day at a time. Consistency is the key. Starting with these recipes, you will be on your way to a much healthier life.

the mission of sugar-free mom recipes

If you've picked up this cookbook you must be looking for a change: ways to feed yourself and your family delicious meals and desserts with less sugar. Everyone knows sugar consumption is out of control and childhood obesity is on the rise. Many diseases feed off of sugar and sugar can make an illness worse. Some even believe as I do, that sugar can be an addiction. Maybe you are just sick and tired and need a complete overhaul to remove sugar and begin your healthy journey. Wherever you are in life, reducing or eliminating sugar will do you a world of good.

Just recognizing the need to reduce is a key component in a healthier lifestyle. If you have children, teaching them by example is the only way to help them desire a healthy life too. Walk the walk, don't just talk the talk. My family still consumes sugar from time to time in moderation, but I would never forbid them from having it in their own diets. I believe forbidding them would make them just rebel and want it more. I've tried to find a balance while raising my three children and feel they are growing up learning to enjoy a balance without an addiction. Unfortunately for me, I was addicted. I will not and cannot ever bring processed sugar or refined flours into my life ever again.

After I conquered my cravings for sugar and really started working on recipes that helped me and my family, my passion grew. Receiving emails and phone calls from friends needing and wanting my recipes was really how it all began. One day my youngest brother suggested I start a blog to collect recipes in one place. Viola! On October 21, 2011, the *Sugar-Free Mom* blog was born.

Before we continue I want to clarify that this cookbook isn't a diet book of low-calorie or even low-fat recipes. In some instances the recipes may certainly be low calorie or low fat, but that is not the mission of this cookbook or these recipes. Cooking and baking without processed sugars is the goal. So, although my recipes may be sugar-free or use natural sugars, not all are not low carb. There is a difference. When recipes are made with fruits, which have natural sugar, the carbs will be higher. My recipes have never been intended for the diabetic, yet some recipes are surely diabetic friendly. Some recipes are low carb, but that is not the first focus. My mission for my children is to reduce the added processed sugars and to use only natural sugars as much as possible. But for myself and maybe for you too, a recipe completely sugar-free is what you are looking for. You will find both types of recipes in this cookbook.

I strive to make sugar-free recipes using stevia and erythritol and develop recipes that both my family and I can enjoy together. Yes, I must limit the honey and natural sweeteners like coconut sugar and even fruits, but I am still able to enjoy them on occasion. I'm not concerned about whether plain Greek yogurt or milks have natural sugars in them. My utmost concern is added sugars.

I've discovered over the last year or so that gluten/wheat is something my body doesn't handle well, so all the recipes now on my blog and in this cookbook are gluten-free. If you're not on a gluten-free diet, I've made recommendations on using whole wheat flours in place of gluten-free flours.

Many of the recipes will also be nut-free, soy-free, and peanut-free due to the allergies of my boys.

natural sugars

Naturally sweet recipes in this cookbook contain some type of natural sugar like bananas or applesauce to sweeten them, along with a little honey, coconut sugar, brown rice syrup, or molasses.

Here's what I've learned about sugar. There are two distinct types:

+ Fructose, which is fruit sugar. Fructose is found in tree and vine fruits, berries, honey, and even root vegetables. This should not be confused with high fructose corn syrup, which is a synthetically manufactured product.

+ Sucrose, which is processed refined sugar. Other names are white refined sugar, cane sugar, brown sugar, powdered sugar, and beet sugar.

Fructose is broken down more slowly in your body. Sucrose is quickly broken down, which increases glucose or blood sugar in your body. We do need glucose since it is a major source of energy for our bodies, but it needs to stay balanced throughout the day, otherwise you experience those rushes of energy and then exhaustion after ingesting a refined sugary treat. When your body senses an increase of glucose in your blood it immediately directs the pancreas to push insulin into the blood stream. Basically, high concentrations of sugar cause blood sugar to be greatly affected. Obviously this is dangerous for someone who is prediabetic or a diabetic since they struggle regulating insulin.

Aside from added sugars, diabetics have trouble processing all glucose coming from foods, such as glucose in carbohydrates. Simple carbohydrates have either added or natural sugars in them. Examples would be fruits, which have fructose, and milks, which have a naturally occurring sugar called lactose. Processed junk foods are also simple carbohydrates, but they have added sugars from sucrose or high fructose corn syrup. The obvious better choice is to have fruit, since it has both fructose and fiber. Complex carbohydrates come from foods like potatoes, rice, breads, and pasta. All carbohydrates enter your bloodstream the same way sugar does. For people who are diabetic, their bodies are unable to produce enough insulin to absorb the glucose from the digested carbohydrates efficiently. This can cause drastically high amounts of glucose in their blood, which can lead to many serious conditions like heart disease, blindness, and kidney failure.

Although I am not a diabetic, my blood sugar is greatly affected when ingesting high amounts of sucrose. When my blood sugar is affected I am irritable, angry, hungry, and craving everything in sight. I don't like that feeling all that much and choose to avoid it at all costs. I believe some people have no problem ingesting sucrose, but for me it just doesn't work.

Here are some of the natural sugars I use in my recipes for my family, but that I limit for myself.

honey

Honey contains about 50 percent fructose and only 1 percent sucrose. The darker the honey, the more nutrients it has. It is the least processed of sugars. About ½ cup of honey equals 1 cup of sugar as far as sweetness is concerned.

coconut palm sugar

Pure coconut palm sugar is a natural sugar made from the nectar of the coconut palm tree. When purchasing coconut palm sugar make sure it is certified 100 percent pure and organic, because many products sold today may also use regular white sugar as a filler. It's low on the glycemic index, which means it won't raise your blood sugar as other sugars do. It is made up of about 70 percent sucrose, but it is less processed and retains a good amount of potassium, magnesium, zinc, and iron.

brown rice syrup

Brown rice syrup, also known as rice syrup or rice malt, is made from rice starch, which is often used in Asian cooking. It contains trace amounts of vitamins and minerals. I've noticed it's the mildest in sweetness of liquid sugars but can be used to replace honey. It is also low on the glycemic index, which means it will enter the bloodstream much slower than other sugars.

black strap molasses

Molasses is derived from sugarcane and is very nutritious. It's rich in iron, also providing calcium, copper, magnesium, manganese, potassium, selenium, and vitamin B. It contains about 25 percent fructose and 55 percent sucrose.

sucanat

Sucanat, sometimes called evaporated cane juice, is not common to most people but is a great substitute to using brown sugar in a recipe. It's made from evaporated sugarcane juice and molasses. It's not commercially processed but instead hand-paddled to dry it. It's about 88 percent sucrose compared to table sugar, which is 99 percent. It browns nicely and works pretty much the same in baking. It ranks as one of the highest in nutritional value because it retains vitamins and minerals found in the sugar cane plant.

maple syrup

Maple syrup is basically 99 percent sucrose. I don't use it for myself at all because it spikes my blood sugar very quickly and I feel the negative effects that often result in sugar cravings. I do allow my children to add it to their pancakes, but I make sure to buy only pure maple syrup.

sugar-free alternatives

erythritol

You may never have heard of this and it might certainly sound like a chemical, but it's not. Erythritol is a sugar alcohol found naturally in fruits. It is about 70 percent as sweet as table sugar. It does not have the same effects on the body as other sugar alcohols like xylitol and maltitol, which can cause laxative effects. Only about 10 percent of erythritol is absorbed in the colon; the rest is excreted unchanged. It is not often associated with digestion issues as other sugar alcohols are. The best part is that it can be used cup for cup in replacing sugar in recipes. Just know that ½ cup of erythritol is not going to provide the same sweetness as ½ cup of typical table sugar would. The end result might be a less sweet dessert than you are used to. It does not raise blood sugar and therefore is perfectly safe for diabetics. Since erythritol can provide the bulk that sugar would have provided in a recipe and stevia is sweeter but doesn't have bulk to it, I like to combine both stevia and erythritol in some dessert recipes for a perfectly sweet result.

stevia

Stevia is derived from a plant in Paraguay. It is a naturally sugar-free plant, but it is 300 times sweeter than sugar. Stevia leaves are dried and a process of water extraction is involved to produce the various forms of stevia seen on market shelves today. Depending on the process of extraction, some brands of stevia will have a bitter aftertaste. I have written about the brands I use and love on my blog so please refer there for the ones I feel produce the best results in my recipes.

Most of my recipes include the following types of stevia:

- **liquid stevia**
- **powdered stevia**
- **pure stevia extract**

There are many types of flavored liquid stevia that include a small amount of natural extracts to enhance flavor, such as lemon, coconut, vanilla, chocolate, orange, and so on. The liquid form of stevia is and has been my number one way to sweeten a recipe. This is often because flavored liquid stevia is fabulous, especially in a no-bake recipe. When you only need a ¼ cup or less of "sugar," I would use these.

Powdered stevia packets are wonderful to take on the go for easy traveling and are great to put in coffee and oatmeal. If you're baking though, you may need to use quite a few in a recipe needing at least a ½ cup of sugar.

Powdered stevia that comes in a bottle and is *not* labeled as an extract often contains inulin fiber. Inulin fiber is a naturally occurring carbohydrate found in 36,000 species of plants. Its most common form comes from chicory. It has health benefits that help increase calcium absorption. It does not raise blood sugar and is suitable for diabetics. Depending on how much inulin fiber is used in any stevia product you purchase, the inulin fiber will render the stevia bland to subtly sweet. Many of my recipes use powdered stevia. I started using this one at the very beginning of my baking with stevia since I was uncertain I wanted to begin with the pure extract. Unless noted in the recipe as pure extract, you would *not* replace pure stevia extract with powdered stevia that contains fiber. The two are not equal in strength, as you will see below. This product could be used in exchange with packets of stevia, since they are about equal in strength.

Pure stevia extract contains no fillers or fiber and you must use very little or you will have a bitter aftertaste in a recipe. Unless a recipe needs you to replace at least a cup of sugar with stevia, I would not recommend using the pure extract. With anything less than a cup, the liquid, packets, or powdered product should be used.

Most stevia baking blends on the market contain maltodextrin. Usually made from rice, corn, or potato starch, maltodextrin is produced by cooking down the starch. It is a processed additive. It is considered safe by the FDA, but that doesn't mean it's healthy. It is basically a filler with no nutritional value. It is one of the first two ingredients in Splenda.

A baking blend of stevia may actually contain sugar or Splenda in it, so it is not something I use and would not be a proper substitute for stevia in these recipes. The benefit of baking blends is you can use it easily to replace a white sugar recipe since it is 1 for 1 and adds bulk, but these recipes have the bulk added in other ways, using applesauce, other fruit purees, and even Greek yogurt. Stevia baking blends are *not* the same as the powdered stevia above and should not be used interchangeably.

For more information on natural sugars and sugar-free alternatives, see the following magazines, books, and websites:

- *Great Life Cuisine Magazine*, November 1998
- *The Low GI Shopper's Guide to GI Values 2014*, by Jennie Brand-Miller, Kaye Foster-Powell, and Fiona Atkinson
- "Stevia: The 'Holy Grail' of Sweetners?" http://articles.mercola.com/sites/articles/archive/2008/12/16/stevia-the-holy-grail-of-sweeteners.aspx
- "America's Deadliest Sweetner Betrays Millions, then Hoodwinks You with Name Change," http://www.huffingtonpost.com/dr-mercola/americas-deadliest-sweete_b_630549.html
- "How Sugar Substitutes Stack Up," http://news.nationalgeographic.com/news/2013/07/130717-sugar-substitutes-nutrasweet-splenda-stevia-baking/
- "The Effects of Brown Rice Syrup on Blood Sugar," http://www.livestrong.com/article/474520-the-effects-of-brown-rice-syrup-on-blood-sugar/
- "The Truth about 'Natural' Sweeteners," http://www.sparkpeople.com/resource/nutrition_articles.asp?id=1203
- "Nutrition of Pure Maple Syrup vs. Honey," http://www.livestrong.com/article/412144-nutrition-of-pure-maple-syrup-vs-honey/
- "Pure Maple Syrup Nutrition," http://www.livestrong.com/article/270564-pure-maple-syrup-nutrition/
- Or see *Wikipedia* for information on the following items: maple syrup, erythritol, stevia, and coconut sugar.

how to purchase the best stevia

Not all stevia products are created equal. Looking for ones that do not contain any additives can be tricky and using certain products with those additives may keep you from enjoying stevia. Many products include additives and the aftertaste can be very strong. Many also have laxative effects when you consume them. Steer away from products whose ingredients list any of the following words: maltodextrin, dextrose, maltitol, sucrose, and sorbitol.

Here's a chart that breaks down what to use if you do not have the right stevia on hand for a recipe.

1 tablespoon powdered	½ cup sugar
10 packets	1 tablespoon powdered stevia
1 teaspoon liquid	1 tablespoon powdered
5 full droppers of liquid	1 teaspoon liquid
¼ teaspoon pure stevia extract	2 tablespoons powdered stevia
½ teaspoon pure stevia extract	2 cups sugar

pantry

Aside from the above-mentioned natural sugars and sugar-free alternatives, the following ingredients will be used to make many of my recipes.

- arrowroot powder
- brown rice
- brown rice flour
- chia seeds
- coconut butter
- coconut flour
- coconut milk
- coconut oil
- extra-virgin olive oil
- flaxseeds
- gluten-free flour blends

- nut butters
- quinoa
- rolled and quick oats
- potato starch
- sugar-free chocolate chips sweetened with stevia or erythritol
- sunflower seed butter
- tapioca starch or flour
- unsweetened baking chocolate
- unsweetened cocoa powder
- xanthan gum

my kitchen essentials

Obvious basic tools, which if you love to cook you likely already have most of, are of course a great set of knives, pot, pans, measuring cups, spoons, a food scale, and a grater for grating zest. To have the most success with some of the recipes in this cookbook you will also need the following:

- A stand mixer (I have a KitchenAid)
- A food processor

- A high-powdered blender
- A slow cooker (crock pot)

how to reduce your sugar consumption

Before you can start revamping your family's lives you must ask yourself some important questions:

- **Will this be a family adventure or will it just be you going sugar-free?**
- **Do you have the support of your spouse?**
- **How much sugar are you and your family really consuming?**
- **Have you ever tried to eat less sugar and what were the results? Reluctance or disapproval from your children or spouse?**

Deciding on whether this adventure will be a family affair or not is your call. It might be easier for you to begin with yourself than the whole family, especially if they aren't used to all natural sugars. Either way start with removing all processed sugars and only buy products or make desserts with some of the natural sweeteners suggested. Avoid all products that use refined flours and choose whole grains instead. Once the family is used to these changes, you can start experimenting with some more sugar-free recipes.

Learning to enjoy baked goods without sugar does take some time. It isn't ever going to match a white flour, white sugar–laden dessert. In time, and with consistent effort to reduce the amount of sugar in your life, baked treats made sugar-free will make you just as happy. Start with the recipes here in this cookbook that contain natural sugars in addition to stevia, which is naturally sugar-free. Beginning this way will provide a gradual change for your family and they may not notice much of a difference at all. You will actually be helping them change their taste buds to prefer less-sweet foods.

Here are some steps to take to start reducing sugar in your family's lives and hopefully get them on board with this new lifestyle change:

1. **Natural Sugars v. Sugar-Free Options**—You must decide which natural sugars you will allow yourself and your family to have and which sugar-free substitutes you want to try. Once you make that decision, the rest will fall into place. Only allow products that contain those natural sugars or sugar-free options in your home.

2. **Become a Food Label Expert**—You *must* read the label on everything that is store bought: from salad dressings, cereals, sauces, and yogurts to dried seasonings for chicken and pretty much everything. Follow the rule that if you find any type of sugar listed within the first 5 ingredients, you just won't buy it or bring it home. You must also look for words like wheat flour, enriched wheat flour, semolina, and durum wheat flour because all of these are actually just white refined flour stripped of all its nutrients. Essentially white refined flour turns to sugar in your body, so if you only get rid of added sugars and don't remove white flour in products, you will still crave sugar. Purchasing whole grains is the better choice. If you want to eat whole grains, look for whole wheat, whole rye, whole barely, and so on, because they have fiber and are digested slower. If the phrase does not begin with *whole*, don't purchase it. Don't be fooled by whole durum semolina or whole enriched wheat flour either; it's still white refined flour. If you are gluten-free, you cannot have wheat, but most gluten-free products use whole foods like brown rice, quinoa, chickpeas, and black beans.

3. **Clean Out Your Pantry**—Go through everything in your cupboards and again look at the labels. If you're happy with the family finishing off what's there, fine, but choose not to bring more into the house. It can be and is quite tempting when prepackaged snacks are available in the cupboard; the kids will almost always choose that over a piece of fruit.

4. **Watch Your Beverages**—Same rules apply to reading labels on beverages as to reading labels for packaged

products. What will your children and you drink? Diet soda isn't any better with all the artificial ingredients in it, so making homemade Fake-Out Fruit Punch (p. 133) and Lemonade (p. 141) is a better option.

5. Start Cooking & Baking—Once your pantry is cleaned out you will need to start replenishing it with snack options your family will enjoy. Take some time on the weekend to prepare ahead some snacks and treats for the week. It is a task worth every bit of your time.

how to curb sugar cravings

Sugar cravings are real. Your body and flesh will fight you hard as soon as you try to withdraw from the treats you are used to. Some people have even shared that they felt as though they had the flu; fatigue, aches, headaches, and other symptoms. How long these symptoms last will depend on how much sugar is truly in your body and how dependent your body is on having sugar on a daily basis. I can only say that as you consistently deny your body the sugar it wants, it does get easier. You may come to the point where you don't even want those treats anymore, as I have done. Once you start trying healthier options, if you go back to something you used to eat regularly you will notice how unbearably sweet and unhealthy it truly tastes. Congratulations, you'll have changed your taste buds!

+ Limit natural sugars to no more than twice a day, even fruits. Sometimes just eliminating the sweet natural foods for a short time with a focus on proteins and veggies will help decrease your cravings for sugar. So when you do have a piece of fruit it will taste like candy to you (well maybe not candy, but you get the point).

+ Reduce or eliminate carbohydrates (bread, rice, pasta, crackers, and so on). Essentially, these types of carbohydrates turn to sugar in your body, which makes you crave more and more each time, never truly feeling satisfied. I limit these to once a week and when I do have them they are things like my oatmeal bread in this cookbook, or brown rice pasta, or rice.

+ Take multivitamins and Omega 3 fish oils. I believe no matter how terrific and balanced you think you eat, everyone can't get all the vitamins and minerals they need from food alone so multivitamins are necessary and important. Omega 3 fish oils help raise the serotonin in your body, which controls your appetite and mood. You can purchase capsules at your local health food store or online. Flaxseeds are also a good source of omega 3.

+ Sleep more. When you don't sleep enough you're tired during the day. When your body is tired, you try to wake it up and often that results in eating more sugar and carbohydrates and in drinking coffee. Try to skip the afternoon munchies and coffee with a recipe like my chia seed pudding, which is full of fiber and protein, and head to bed an hour earlier than usual to catch up on sleep.

+ Find alternatives to your favorite treats that won't raise your blood sugar, such as the recipes in this cookbook.

+ Eat peanut butter or another higher-fat food, like an avocado. Whenever I am really craving a piece of chocolate or some carbohydrates I eat a spoonful of peanut butter and it calms me down. Fat is satiating. But if I really want chocolate, I make my own super food chocolate bar!

+ Exercise. I've said this before and I will say it again, I'm always one workout away from a good mood. I mean that exercise is as much for my emotions as it is for my body. It keeps me balanced and it helps release happy hormones. When I work out I want to eat better and take care of myself. If you are craving sugar, get out of the house and go for a walk!

+ Find a buddy. Going it alone is hard. I've tried it both ways and having a buddy is better! This is someone you can call who can relate to your struggle and can lend positive, uplifting encouragement when you are down.

recipe labels in this cookbook

All the recipes include nutritional information that is calculated per serving. If you are a diabetic, it is most important that you look at the net carbohydrate grams, not so much at the sugars in these recipes. Net carbohydrate grams can be found by subtracting the fiber from the total carbohydrate grams in the recipe per serving. A recipe labeled "low carbohydrate" will have 12 net grams or less of carbohydrates. Recipes that have 1 gram or less of sugar are considered sugar-free.

Low Carbohydrate

Natural Sugar

Sugar-Free

Dairy-Free

My hope is that through the recipes in this cookbook you will be able to achieve your desired freedom from sugar. You will realize that eating less or no sugar doesn't mean having to feel like you are missing out on what others are enjoying. Having a passion to cook and eat doesn't have to stop just because sugar isn't in your life. I hope you enjoy these wholesome, natural recipes with your family and friends, sharing meals and treats together, cooking in the kitchen and creating memories, and most importantly, sharing the message that a sugar-free lifestyle is not only possible without deprivation, but truly enjoyable as well.

~Brenda

breakfast

personal-sized baked oatmeal cups

This recipe is near and dear to my heart. As a way to please everyone in the family, but still make one recipe, this idea was created. Making one large baked oatmeal never worked for my family. If I made it with berries, one child wouldn't eat it. Hubby wanted nuts, but the boys are allergic. I wanted it plain, but no one would eat it that way. Muffin-sized baked oatmeal with individual toppings came to mind and I soared with it. My picky teen hates all things oatmeal but loves these. The little man says, "It's like eating cake for breakfast, Mommy!" And the readers of my blog have loved this recipe; it was and still is the recipe that took my blog viral, continuing to be my number one traffic source since February 2012 when it was first published.

2 eggs

1 tsp. vanilla extract

2 cups applesauce, unsweetened

1 banana, mashed (½ cup)

6 packets of stevia or 1½ tsp. pure stevia extract or ½ cup honey

5 cups rolled oats

2 Tbsp. ground flaxseeds

1 Tbsp. ground cinnamon

3 tsp. baking powder

1 tsp. salt

2¼ cups milk, 1%

optional toppings: raisins, walnuts, chocolate chips, trail mix, dried cranberries, coconut

1. Preheat oven to 350 degrees. Mix eggs, vanilla, applesauce, banana, and stevia together in a bowl. Add in oats, flax, cinnamon, baking powder, and salt, and mix well with wet ingredients. Finally, add milk and combine.

2. Spray a 12- and a 6-capacity muffin tin with cooking spray or use cupcake liners. Pour mixture evenly into muffin tin cups. If using toppings, add onto tops of oatmeal cups now. If using fresh or frozen fruit, press into individual oatmeal cups.

3. Bake 30 minutes or until a toothpick in center comes out clean. Cool and enjoy or freeze in gallon freezer bags.

makes 18 servings

nutritional information

Calories: 144 ◆ Fat: 3 g ◆ Sat. Fat: .6 g ◆ Cholesterol: 21 mg ◆ Sodium: 154 mg ◆ Carbs: 22.9 g ◆ Fiber: 3.3 g ◆ Sugars: 2.7 g ◆ Protein: 6 g

banana bread 🅝🅢 🅓🅕 *(sub with dairy-free milk)*

My family loves banana bread. My mother and grandmother have been making it for years and would often bring a loaf over when I moved out on my own. Once I decided that sugar couldn't be part of my life I thought that meant the end of good banana bread. Nope, I was wrong. My blog has the whole wheat version, but for this cookbook I wanted the gluten-free version since that is how I bake for myself now. Since this contains natural sugar from bananas it's a healthy choice for us moms who want to reduce how much refined sugar our family consumes.

2 eggs

1 tsp. vanilla extract

½ cup milk, 1%

½ cup applesauce

1 tsp. vanilla liquid stevia

3 bananas, mashed

2 cups gluten-free flour (my blend uses brown rice flour)

1 Tbsp. flaxseeds

½ tsp. salt

1 tsp. baking powder

1 tsp. baking soda

1 tsp. ground cinnamon

1 tsp. xanthan gum

1. Preheat oven to 350 degrees. Blend first 6 ingredients in a blender. Set aside. Whisk dry ingredients together in a large bowl. Blend wet into dry ingredients.

2. Pour batter into a loaf pan and bake 60 minutes or until golden brown and a toothpick in center comes out clean.

Makes 16 pieces

nutritional information

Calories: 89 ♦ Fat: 1.4 g ♦ Sat. Fat: .2 g ♦ Cholesterol: 23 mg ♦ Sodium: 87 mg ♦ Carbs: 17.5 g ♦ Fiber: 2.4 g ♦ Sugars: 3.8 g ♦ Protein: 3 g

oatmeal seed bread

Sometimes after a hard workout with weights at the gym in the morning, I come home and I am hungry! I need something hearty, and for me, this is it. I toast up two slices, add some cream cheese or peanut butter, and have some hardboiled egg whites on the side. Then I'm satisfied. Not low fat, but healthy fats in seeds will keep you satiated. Quite a lot of proteins in one slice as well.

1 cup plus 1 Tbsp. raw pumpkin seeds, divided

1 cup plus 1 Tbsp. raw sunflower seeds, divided

½ cup plus 1 Tbsp. rolled oats, divided

1 cup flaxseeds

¼ tsp. pure stevia extract

½ tsp. salt

2 tsp. baking powder

1 tsp. ground cinnamon

½ tsp. nutmeg

4 eggs, beaten

½ cup unsweetened almond milk

½ tsp. vanilla extract

1. Preheat oven to 350 degrees. In a food processor, process 1 cup pumpkin seeds, 1 cup sunflower seeds, ½ cup rolled oats, flaxseeds, stevia, salt, baking powder, cinnamon, and nutmeg.

2. Add eggs, milk, and vanilla, and blend until combined.

3. Pour mixture into a parchment-lined loaf pan. Sprinkle over top 1 tablespoon each of pumpkin seeds, sunflower seeds, and rolled oats. Bake 55–60 minutes or until a skewer comes out clean in center.

makes 14 servings

nutritional information

Calories: 185 ◆ Fat: 13.7 g ◆ Sat. Fat: 2 g ◆ Cholesterol: 51 mg ◆ Sodium: 108 mg ◆ Carbs: 8 g ◆ Fiber: 5.1 g ◆ Sugars: .1 g ◆ Protein: 9.3 g

blueberry refrigerator jam

If you're not much into canning jelly or jams (I'm not), this recipe will be a godsend to you. Chia seeds give the jam a perfect consistency typical of a regular store-bought version. You can experiment with any berries you like; blackberries, strawberries, and raspberries would be fantastic here. Since changing the sweetener is always an option, just taste and adjust to your liking. If berries are frozen, thaw first and then drain juices.

3 cups blueberries, fresh or frozen

2 Tbsp. water

1 Tbsp. powdered stevia

2 tsp. vanilla liquid extract

1 pinch salt

1 tsp. vanilla liquid stevia

1 Tbsp. lemon juice

¼ cup chia seeds

1. In a blender, place blueberries and water and pulse until mixture reaches desired consistency.

2. Add stevia, vanilla, salt, vanilla stevia, and lemon juice, and pulse again. Pour blueberry mixture into a bowl and stir in chia seeds. Pour mixture into mason jars and refrigerate for an hour to gel. Makes 24 ounces.

makes 12 servings @ 2 Tbsp. per serving

nutritional information

Calories: 22 ◆ Fat: .8 g ◆ Sat. Fat: .1 g ◆ Cholesterol: 0 mg ◆ Sodium: 0 mg ◆ Carbs: 3.4 g ◆ Fiber: 1.3 g ◆ Sugars: 1.6 g ◆ Protein: .6 g

grain-free chocolate glazed donuts

Let's be honest, kids like donuts. Whenever I make a trip to get a coffee my kids want a donut. I rarely let them, but on occasion the hubby or auntie brings some home to them. I tried a few combinations of flours to get the right texture for these and finally, after quite a few unsuccessful attempts with a so-so donut, these baked goodies are for the win. If you want a sweeter donut, make sure to use the 2 teaspoons of stevia. My little man hates the flavor of coconut flour, but in these it's unrecognizable. You just taste the chocolate goodness.

½ cup coconut flour

½ cup unsweetened cocoa powder

1 tsp. baking powder

¼ tsp. baking soda

½ cup erythritol or 3 Tbsp. powdered stevia

½ tsp. salt

½ cup milk, 1%

¼ cup plain Greek yogurt, 2%

4 eggs

2 Tbsp. oil

1 tsp. vanilla extract

1-2 tsp. vanilla liquid stevia

chocolate glaze

¼ cup sugar-free chocolate chips

2 Tbsp. butter

1. Preheat oven to 350 degrees. Spray or grease a donut pan.

2. Whisk dry ingredients together. Blend wet ingredients together in a separate bowl. Slowly stir dry ingredients into wet until combined. Pour into donut pan, filling each halfway.

3. Bake 15 minutes or until donuts bounce back when touched or toothpick near center comes out clean. Remove from donut pan and cool on wire rack.

4. Once cool, melt glaze ingredients in microwave for 30 seconds and stir until smooth. Evenly pour over the top of each donut.

makes 9 donuts

nutritional information

Calories: 202 ◆ Fat: 15.1 g ◆ Sat. Fat: 6.7 g ◆ Cholesterol: 95 mg ◆ Sodium: 199 mg ◆ Carbs: 15.3 g ◆ Fiber: 6.1 g ◆ Sugars: .3 g ◆ Protein: 6.8 g

blueberry lemon scones

Making scones always seemed like a lot of work to me, but honestly they are anything but. A simple dough comes together quickly using a food processor, a bit of kneading, making into a circle, cutting, and baking! Frozen blueberries would also work here, but you would need to thaw and drain before using.

1 cup fresh blueberries

2 cups gluten-free flour

1 tsp. baking powder

1 Tbsp. powdered stevia

1 tsp. xanthan gum

½ tsp. salt

½ tsp. cream of tartar

6 Tbsp. cold butter

1 egg

¾ cup milk, 1%

½ tsp. lemon liquid stevia

juice of ½ lemon or 2 tsp.

½ tsp. lemon zest or ½ lemon

1 Tbsp. water

topping

½ tsp. lemon juice

zest of ½ lemon

1 egg white

1 tsp. powdered stevia or 1 Tbsp. erythritol

1. Preheat oven to 425 degrees. Wash and dry blueberries and let stand on paper towels. Set aside.

2. Whisk together flour, baking powder, powdered stevia, xanthan gum, salt, and cream of tartar. Cut butter into flour mixture with two knives or use a food processor to pulse until flour is the size of peas. Fold in blueberries.

3. In a separate bowl whisk together egg, milk, lemon stevia, lemon juice, and lemon zest. Make a well in the flour mixture and pour in the milk mixture. Add water and stir until a dough forms. With floured hands knead dough on a floured surface. Then place dough onto a parchment-lined baking sheet.

4. Roll dough into an 8-inch circle. With an oiled pizza cutter, slice 8 slices. Separate with an oiled spatula so the scone triangles are not touching. Mix the topping ingredients in a small bowl and use a pastry brush to brush topping onto each scone. Bake for 20 minutes.

makes 8 servings

nutritional information

Calories: 208 ♦ Fat: 10.5 g ♦ Sat. Fat: 4.6 g ♦ Cholesterol: 46 mg ♦ Sodium: 235 mg ♦ Carbs: 25.9 g ♦ Fiber: 3.4 g ♦ Sugars: 2.8 g ♦ Protein: 5.4 g

baked french toast sticks

Breakfasts are always a challenge when you have a picky family. Making french toast sticks for my kids is one of the ways I combat those crazy hectic days. I freeze them ahead and the kids can easily place them in the toaster to reheat. Everyone is happy!

3 eggs

½ cup milk, 1%

2 tsp. vanilla extract

2½ tsp. ground cinnamon, divided

8 slices (16 oz.) sprouted grain loaf bread, crusts cut off and cut into 16 sticks (¾ inch thick)

2 Tbsp. coconut sugar, divided

2 Tbsp. butter, melted

1. Whisk eggs, milk, vanilla, and 2 teaspoons cinnamon together in a bowl. Soak bread sticks in egg mixture for a few minutes on each side and place on a lined baking sheet.

2. Preheat oven to 350 degrees. Stir together remaining ½ teaspoon of cinnamon with 1 tablespoon coconut sugar. Sprinkle sticks with coconut sugar and cinnamon mixture and bake 10 minutes. Flip sticks over, sprinkle 1 more tablespoon coconut sugar and drizzle butter over sticks. Bake another 10 minutes.

makes 4 servings @ 4 sticks per serving

nutritional information

Calories: 306 ◆ Fat: 10.1 g ◆ Sat. Fat: 3.9 g ◆ Cholesterol: 152 mg ◆ Sodium: 258 mg ◆ Carbs: 37.8 g ◆ Fiber: 6 g ◆ Sugars: .1 g ◆ Protein: 14 g

cinnamon coconut flour pancakes   *(sub with dairy-free milk)*

I was taking a chance when I made these coconut flour pancakes for the first time with my little man. He is not the fan of anything coconut in flavor. With the addition of cinnamon and my favorite vanilla stevia, he had no idea and ate 3 pancakes before asking what they were made of. The picky teen and dear daughter, as well as my picky husband, were pleased and content with these pancakes. Easy to make ahead and keep all week in the fridge for easy, stress-free mornings.

4 eggs

1 cup milk, 1%

2 tsp. vanilla extract

½ cup coconut flour

1 tsp. ground cinnamon

½ tsp. ground nutmeg

1 tsp. vanilla liquid stevia

½ tsp. salt

1 tsp. baking soda

2 tsp. powdered stevia

2 Tbsp. coconut oil

1. Mix all ingredients except coconut oil together in a high powdered blender. Set aside.

2. Heat coconut oil on a griddle pan and ladle ¼ cup batter onto griddle for each pancake. Cook until pancake edges look set and center bubbles. Flip over and cook a few minutes on other side.

makes 8 pancakes

nutritional information (one pancake):

Calories: 110 ◆ Fat: 6.6 g ◆ Sat. Fat: 4.2 g ◆ Cholesterol: 91 mg ◆ Sodium: 193 mg ◆ Carbs: 6.8 g ◆ Fiber: 3 g ◆ Sugars: .2 g ◆ Protein: 5.4 g

belgian waffles

Make-ahead waffles for the school week mornings is another time-saving recipe. I love to refrigerate a few batches or freeze them, and then the kids help themselves by reheating them in the toaster oven. You could use whole wheat flour in place of the gluten-free flour. My daughter likes to make waffle sandwiches out of these with bananas and peanut butter.

1½ cups gluten-free flour

2 tsp. baking powder

½ tsp. salt

½ tsp. pure stevia extract

1 Tbsp. oil (I used olive oil)

4 eggs, separated

1 tsp. vanilla extract

2 Tbsp. butter, softened

2 cups milk, 1%

1. Heat waffle iron according to manufacturer's directions. Mix first 4 ingredients together and set aside.

2. In a bowl whisk oil, egg yolks, vanilla extract, butter, and milk. Set aside. In a stand mixer, beat egg whites until they resemble whipped cream. Add wet ingredients into dry until just blended. Using a rubber spatula, fold egg whites into batter.

3. Spray waffle iron or grease it. Makes 6 belgian waffles.

makes 12 servings @ 1/2 a waffle per serving

nutritional information

Calories: 121 ◆ Fat: 5.4 g ◆ Sat. Fat: 1.8 g ◆ Cholesterol: 67 mg ◆ Sodium: 154 mg ◆ Carbs: 13.4 g ◆ Fiber: 1.5 g ◆ Sugars: .5 g ◆ Protein: 5.2 g

cinnamon granola with nut-free option

My hubby and I absolutely love a good, nutty granola, but often I make it nut-free so my little man can enjoy some as well. Just replace the mixed nuts with pumpkin seeds or sunflower seeds, increase the rolled oats, or add more coconut if you like, even some dried fruit. Granola will never be a low-calorie recipe due to the oats and nuts, but this version has considerably less sugar than any you could purchase.

2 cups roughly chopped almonds, walnuts, pecans, and hazelnuts (½ cup of each)

2 cups rolled oats

¼ cup coconut oil

⅓ cup coconut sugar

1 tsp. vanilla extract

1 tsp. ground cinnamon

½ tsp. salt

1 tsp. vanilla liquid stevia

1 cup unsweetened coconut flakes

1. Preheat oven to 350 degrees. Place nuts (or seeds) and oats in a bowl. Set aside.

2. Melt coconut oil and coconut sugar together with vanilla extract, cinnamon, salt, and vanilla liquid stevia over low heat in a saucepan. Bring to a gentle boil and then pour mixture into bowl with nuts/seeds and oats. Stir well to coat.

3. Spread nuts/seeds and oats onto a greased baking sheet. Bake 10 minutes and stir well. Then mix in coconut flakes and bake another 10–15 minutes or until golden brown. Cool and break into pieces and store in an airtight container.

makes about 5 cups @ ½ cup per serving

nutritional information

Calories: 356 ♦ Fat: 26.2 g ♦ Sat. Fat: 10.8 g ♦ Cholesterol: 0 mg ♦ Sodium: 125 mg ♦ Carbs: 25.4 g ♦ Fiber: 5.3 g ♦ Sugars: 1.3 g ♦ Protein: 6.7 g

no-bake nut-free granola bars

Oh the plight of moms whose children have nut allergies. Some are not as severe as others, but they still make a difficult task of buying anything prepackaged. These are the easiest no-bake granola bars that use only a small amount of honey to sweeten them. It's a nutritious bar packed full of healthy ingredients. You can change out the seeds for nuts if you have no problem with them in your family. But this is a great nut-free alternative to bring to school. Creamed honey is much thicker than typical honey. If you don't have that you could substitute brown rice syrup.

1 cup crispy brown rice cereal

¾ cup rolled oats

½ cup unsweetened shredded coconut

¼ cup unsweetened cocoa powder

¼ cup ground flaxseeds

¼ cup sunflower seeds

2 packets powdered stevia or ½ tsp. pure stevia extract

2 Tbsp. pumpkin seeds, divided

2 Tbsp. sugar-free chocolate chips, divided

⅓ cup coconut butter

⅓ cup creamed clover honey

¼ cup coconut oil

1 tsp. vanilla extract

1. Combine the first 7 ingredients together in a large bowl. Add 1 tablespoon pumpkin seeds and 1 tablespoon chocolate chips. Save the rest for topping the bars.

2. Combine coconut butter, honey, coconut oil, and vanilla extract, and melt together in the microwave for 1 minute or over the stove on low heat until melted and stirred to combine. Pour wet ingredients into dry and combine well.

3. Line an 8 × 8 baking dish with parchment paper that extends over the sides for easy grasping to remove later. Spray or grease the parchment. Spread mixture onto the parchment paper and level with a spatula. Sprinkle remaining pumpkin seeds and chocolate chips over the top and press into mixture.

4. Refrigerate 30 minutes and then remove by holding the ends of the parchment paper and place onto a cutting board to slice. They do not need to be kept refrigerated. Wrap individually for packing/storing. Good up to 1 week.

makes 16 bars

nutritional information

Calories: 158 ♦ Fat: 11.4 g ♦ Sat. Fat: 7.8 g ♦ Cholesterol: 0 mg ♦ Sodium: 10 mg ♦ Carbs: 14.9 g ♦ Fiber: 3.2 g ♦ Sugars: 5.8 mg ♦ Protein: 2.9 g

coffee cake

I always find coffee cake recipes without any coffee in the ingredient list a little odd. My hubby loves a good coffee cake with his coffee so I went on a mission to make a gluten-free version so I could indulge myself. My kids love coffee cake as well, so using decaffeinated or caffeinated is up to you. This can also be made using whole wheat flour and you can remove the xanthan gum if you choose not to use gluten-free flour.

1 cup gluten-free rolled oats

1 cup gluten-free flour

1 tsp. cinnamon

½ tsp. salt

1 tsp. baking powder

1 tsp. xanthan gum

2 Tbsp. ground flaxseeds

1 tsp. baking soda

2 Tbsp. powdered stevia

2 eggs

1 cup plain Greek yogurt, 2%

¼ cup butter, melted

½ cup chilled brewed coffee

1 tsp. vanilla extract

topping

¼ cup coconut sugar

1 Tbsp. cinnamon

½ cup chopped pecans

¼ cup butter, melted

1. Whisk together first 9 ingredients. Set aside. Beat eggs until frothy and then add yogurt, butter, coffee, and vanilla extract. Blend until combined well. Add dry ingredients slowly into wet ingredients.

2. Preheat oven to 350 degrees. Grease or spray with non-stick cooking spray an 8 × 8 baking pan. Pour half of batter into the pan. Stir together topping ingredients. Spread half over cake batter. Pour remaining cake batter over nut mixture, and then sprinkle remaining topping over that. Bake 40 minutes.

makes 9 pieces

nutritional information

Calories: 264 • Fat: 15.4 g • Sat. Fat: 6 g • Cholesterol: 69 mg • Sodium: 306 mg • Carbs: 25.3 g • Fiber: 3.9 g • Sugars: 1.7 g • Protein: 7.7 g

personalized puff pancakes

Personalized breakfasts are a big hit on my blog mainly because trying to feed picky family members is always tough. I love to be able to make one basic recipe and then customize it for each person with simple toppings. The whole wheat version of these is on my blog and the gluten-free version is equally delicious. Again, if you are not gluten-free, replace the gluten-free flour with the flour of your choice and remove the xanthan gum.

6 eggs

1 cup milk, 1%

1 cup gluten-free flour

½ tsp. xanthan gum

1 tsp. vanilla extract

1 tsp. baking powder

½ tsp. vanilla liquid stevia

toppings

Add 1 tablespoon of any of the following to personal pancakes: frozen or fresh blueberries, raspberries, strawberries, peaches, cherries, unsweetened shredded coconut, or sugar-free chocolate chips. If using frozen fruit, thaw and drain before adding.

1. Preheat oven to 425 degrees. Grease or spray with nonstick cooking spray 6 ramekins. Mix all ingredients together. Evenly pour batter into each ramekin and add toppings as desired to each. Bake 25 minutes or until golden and puffed. Enjoy warm!

makes 6 servings

nutritional information

Calories: 158 ✦ Fat: 5.2 g ✦ Sat. Fat: 1.3 g ✦ Cholesterol: 182 mg ✦ Sodium: 84 mg ✦ Carbs: 17.3 g ✦ Fiber: 2.2 g ✦ Sugars: .7 g ✦ Protein: 9.9 g

crock pot overnight french toast casserole

I'm really not a fan of making french toast because I'd rather just throw something in the oven or crock pot and get other things done off my to-do list. Making a french toast–flavored casserole in the crock pot is as close as my family will have to typical french toast. Simply mix and toss, cover, turn it on, and head to bed! Wake in the morning to a fabulous smell and a breakfast ready. Gotta love that!

6 eggs, slightly beaten

½ cup ricotta cheese

2 cups milk, 1%

1 tsp. vanilla extract

1 tsp. cinnamon

½ tsp. ground cloves

½ tsp. allspice

¼ tsp. ground ginger

¼ tsp. salt

8 packets of powdered stevia or ½ tsp. pure extract

2 tsp. vanilla liquid stevia (10 full droppers)

6 cups cubed gluten-free bread

optional: unsweetened Greek yogurt mixed with stevia to taste

1. Whisk all ingredients together except bread. Spray crock pot on the bottom with nonstick cooking spray or butter the bottom.

2. In a bowl, toss bread with egg mixture. Pour into the crock pot and cook on low 8–9 hours. Add optional toppings if desired.

makes 6 servings

nutritional information

Calories: 249 • Fat: 9 g • Sat. Fat: 2.9 g • Cholesterol: 193 mg • Sodium: 665 mg • Carbs: 26.9 g • Fiber: 2 g • Sugars: 3.7 g • Protein: 13.5 g

personalized overnight oatmeal smoothies

Make one base recipe and personalize it with different add-ins. Make ahead and refrigerate overnight. Grab and go in the morning!

basic smoothie

1½ cups rolled oats

¼ cup plus 2 Tbsp. chia seeds

6 cups milk, 1%

1 cup plain Greek yogurt, 2%

1 Tbsp. vanilla extract

2 tsp. pure stevia extract

add these to each base to personalize

1. Strawberry Banana: ½ cup strawberries, 1 banana

2. Cherry Vanilla: 1 cup frozen or fresh pitted cherries, 1 tsp. vanilla extract

3. Peanut Butter Chocolate: 2 Tbsp. peanut butter, 2 Tbsp. unsweetened cocoa powder

4. Blueberry Coconut: ½ cup blueberries, 2 Tbsp. unsweetened shredded coconut

5. Apple Cinnamon: ½ cup unsweetened applesauce, 2 tsp. ground cinnamon

6. Orange Cranberry: 1 orange, peeled, 2 Tbsp. dried cranberries

1. In a high powdered blender, place rolled oats and chia seeds. Blend on high until the consistency of flour. Pour in milk, yogurt, vanilla extract, and stevia, and blend until completely combined.

2. Pour basic smoothie into 6 mason jars until each is ¾ of the way full. Add personal ingredients into each mason jar. Take one personalized mason jar smoothie and place back into blender and blend until smooth or desired consistency. Pour back into the same mason jar. You may want to rinse the blender before making the next smoothie. Proceed with the rest of the mason jars smoothies. If there are nut allergies in your family make sure to blend the peanut butter smoothie last. Cover and refrigerate overnight. Nutritional information is for the base recipe, not the add-ins.

makes 6 servings

nutritional information

Calories: 296 • Fat: 10.1 g • Sat. Fat: 3 g • Cholesterol: 12 mg • Sodium: 155 mg • Carbs: 34.4 g • Fiber: 7.1 g • Sugars: 1.9 g • Protein: 19.4 g

personalized breakfast pizzas

Breakfast pizza is a favorite for my family. Rather than making one large pizza, individual tortillas work much better for the ability to personalize with whatever toppings each person wants. Make for breakfast or for a quick dinner.

6 small (6-inch) corn tortillas or 3 large (12-inch) brown rice tortillas

6 oz. frozen spinach

6 eggs, beaten

2 egg whites

½ cup milk, 1%

1 Tbsp. coconut oil

6 slices turkey bacon, nitrate-free, cooked crisp and crumbled

1 cup diced sweet peppers

¼ cup diced onion

1 cup shredded cheddar cheese or Mexican blend

1. Bake tortillas in oven at 350 degrees for 3–5 minutes or until crisp. Set aside.

2. Cook frozen spinach in microwave for 3 minutes and then drain out excess water. In a bowl, mix eggs, whites, and milk. In a saucepan over medium heat melt coconut oil and cook eggs, egg whites, and milk. Stir constantly until scrambled.

3. Top each tortilla with scrambled eggs and additional toppings as desired. Finish with cheese and bake in oven for 3 minutes or until cheese is melted. Nutritional information uses 6 small corn tortillas.

makes 6 servings @ 1 (6-inch) tortilla or ½ (12-inch) tortilla per serving

nutritional information

Calories: 325 ◆ Fat: 14.8 g ◆ Sat. Fat: 7.2 g ◆ Cholesterol: 226 mg ◆ Sodium: 624 mg ◆ Carbs: 18.4 g ◆ Fiber: 1.7 g ◆ Sugars: 1.5 g ◆ Protein: 25.7 g

apple pie oat muffins

We love muffins in our house. I think because they are so easy to make and they are perfect for making ahead and taking on the go. This is a family favorite. The original recipe uses whole wheat on my blog, but here they are made gluten-free and have a delicious crumble topping that makes them even better!

1¼ cups rolled oats

1¼ cups brown rice flour

½ tsp. xanthan gum

½ tsp. salt

1 tsp. baking powder

½ tsp. baking soda

1 tsp. ground cinnamon

¼ tsp. ground cardamom

½ tsp. pure stevia extract

2 eggs

1 tsp. vanilla extract

1 cup unsweetened applesauce

¼ cup butter, melted

½ cup milk, 1%

2 apples, peeled, cored, and chopped (about 2 cups)

oat crumble topping

2 Tbsp. gluten-free flour

3 Tbsp. rolled oats

2 Tbsp. butter, softened

1 tsp. ground cinnamon

1 Tbsp. coconut sugar

1. Preheat oven to 400 degrees. Combine all dry ingredients (including spices) together in a bowl. In another bowl whisk together eggs, vanilla extract, applesauce, butter, and milk. Stir apple chunks into wet mixture.

2. Pour wet mixture into dry ingredients and stir to incorporate. Spray or grease a 12-capacity muffin tin. Evenly pour batter into each cup. In a small bowl stir together oat topping ingredients until crumbly and then sprinkle over each muffin. Bake 15 minutes or until a toothpick in center comes out clean.

makes 12 servings

nutritional information

Calories: 195 ◆ Fat: 7.9 g ◆ Sat. Fat: 3.3 g ◆ Cholesterol: 46 mg ◆ Sodium: 209 mg ◆ Carbs: 27.4 g ◆ Fiber: 2.5 g ◆ Sugars: 3.4 g ◆ Protein: 4.6 g

oatmeal breakfast cookies

A cookie for breakfast? Absolutely! The kids may look at you with crazy eyes like you've lost your mind for a minute and then happily inhale a few!

1 cup rolled oats

½ cup ground sunflower seeds

¼ cup nonfat dry milk powder

2 tsp. ground cinnamon

¼ tsp. baking soda

1 egg, beaten

1 large banana, mashed (½ cup)

1 tsp. vanilla extract

½ cup nut butter or sunflower seed butter

¼ cup honey

optional toppings

¼ cup chocolate chips

¼ cup raisins

¼ cup trail mix

¼ cup dried cherries

1. Preheat oven to 350 degrees. Mix dry ingredients together in a bowl. Whisk egg, banana, and vanilla in a separate bowl.

2. Blend honey and nut butter together. Mix nut butter and honey with egg, banana, and vanilla. Add wet ingredients to dry ingredients. Stir until just combined. Divide batter into parts if you'd like different toppings for cookies (especially for those with nut allergies). Make 18 mounds and place them onto a Silpat- or parchment-lined cookie sheet. Add toppings to each mound and, using a spatula dipped in water, flatten toppings into cookies. Bake 15–16 minutes or until browned. Transfer to a wire rack to cool. Freeze up to 3 months or keep in a resalable container for up to 3 days. Nutritional information uses sunflower seed butter and no toppings.

makes 18 cookies

nutritional information

Calories: 96 ◆ Fat: 4.4 g ◆ Sat. Fat: .5 g ◆ Cholesterol: 10 mg ◆ Sodium: 64 mg ◆ Carbs: 11.8 g ◆ Fiber: 1.4 g ◆ Sugars: 5.6 g ◆ Protein: 3.5 g

light bites, salads, sides, and more

mayo-free chicken salad lettuce wraps

This mayo-free chicken salad is a popular recipe on my blog. I have always loved mayonnaise chicken salad, but one day I just decided to use Greek yogurt instead. My hubby, who isn't a mayo fan, loves this recipe more than any other chicken salad he's tried. I've made this for my Italian family at a family reunion last summer and they were in awe that it didn't contain mayo but was still so creamy. The lemon juice really brings the flavors together for a fresh, tasty bite, whether you place it in a lettuce wrap or top a salad with it.

8 oz. cooked chicken breast

2 Tbsp. plain Greek yogurt, full fat

¼ cup fresh cilantro, chopped

2 scallions, chopped

¼ cup thinly diced celery

½ tsp. salt

¼ tsp. pepper

¼ tsp. garlic powder

¼ tsp. cumin

3 Tbsp. lemon juice

½ cup cherry tomatoes, halved

2 butter lettuce leaves, washed and dried

1. Shred chicken in a food processor. Mix chicken with remaining ingredients except tomatoes and lettuce in a bowl. Serve chicken salad in lettuce cups and top with tomatoes. Makes 1 cup.

makes 2 servings

nutritional information

Calories: 150 • Fat: 1.6 g • Sat. Fat: .2 g • Cholesterol: 61 mg • Sodium: 920 mg • Carbs: 5.8 g • Fiber: .9 g • Sugars: 3 g • Protein: 28.9 g

italian sausage & pepper quesadillas

You could certainly use regular Italian sausage or kielbasa even, but if you want to keep it lighter on the fat and calories, Italian turkey sausage is a perfect choice. This is a fast weeknight dinner for the family.

4 links Italian turkey sausage, casings removed

½ tsp. salt

¼ tsp. pepper

1 tsp. Italian seasoning

1 Tbsp. oil

1 garlic clove, minced

½ red onion, sliced

1 red pepper, sliced

2 cups chopped (chiffonade-style) kale (or spinach) with stems removed

1 cup shredded mozzarella

4 whole wheat, whole grain, or gluten-free tortillas

1. Cook sausage in a skillet and break into crumbles until browned. Add salt, pepper, and Italian seasoning. Remove sausage and set aside.

2. Add oil, garlic, onion, and pepper, to skillet and cook until softened. Add kale and cook until wilted. Place sausage in vegetable pan. Divide filling into 4 servings and place in centers of four tortillas. Add ¼ cup mozzarella cheese to each prepared tortilla.

3. Heat a sauté pan, place tortilla in it, and heat until cheese is melted. Fold tortilla in half and flip to crisp other side. Nutritional information uses gluten-free tortillas.

makes 4 servings

nutritional information

Calories: 483 ◆ Fat: 24.7 g ◆ Sat. Fat: 7 g ◆ Cholesterol: 85 mg ◆ Sodium: 1707 mg ◆ Carbs: 38.3 g ◆ Fiber: 4.8 g ◆ Sugars: 2.6 g ◆ Protein: 27.7 g

mini bacon chicken cheddar quinoa bites

If you've not tried quinoa yet, you've got to experience this fantastic gluten-free seed. It's a great substitute for rice in dishes, it's fantastic in salads, and it works well in desserts to substitute flour. I've got mini quinoa brownie bites on my blog that no one would ever notice has quinoa in them. It adds protein and fiber and has a slight nutty flavor, but it really remains neutral and takes on the flavors it's combined with. The best part is that is requires 15 minutes to cook and no draining—a lot quicker than rice. Once cooked you can combine it in a salad, serve it as a side with herbs and spices, or make it like this for the kids. Perfect and easy finger food!

1 cup quinoa, rinsed

2 cups water

1 cup cooked, shredded chicken

½ cup crumbled crispy cooked turkey bacon (about 4 slices)

¾ cup shredded cheddar cheese

2 eggs

3 Tbsp. gluten-free flour

½ tsp. salt

¼ tsp. pepper

2 Tbsp. fresh chopped parsley

¼ cup Mayo-Free Ranch Dressing (p. 118)

1. Preheat oven to 350 degrees. Boil quinoa in water for 12–15 minutes or until all the water is absorbed. Let cool.

2. In a bowl combine remaining ingredients. Add quinoa once cooled and mix well. Grease a mini muffin tin and then fill by pressing mixture into each. Bake for 20 minutes.

makes 8 servings @ 4 mini quinoa bites per serving

nutritional information

Calories: 193 ✦ Fat: 6.6 g ✦ Sat. Fat: 2.1 g ✦ Cholesterol: 80 mg ✦ Sodium: 570 mg ✦ Carbs: 17.5 g ✦ Fiber: 1.8 g ✦ Sugars: .6 g ✦ Protein: 14.8 g

classic pasta fagioli

This is an Italian classic! I've grown up enjoying this soup that my grandmother made each week. She actually never included the ham bone so it was a meatless soup, but since I have a hubby who won't touch a soup without meat in it, meat needed to be added. I can't say it's better than my grandmother's because that would be a disgrace, but it is pretty close!

1 ham bone with meat still on it (or about 2 cups diced cooked ham)

1 (28-oz.) can crushed tomato sauce

3 tsp. minced garlic

1 tsp. pepper

4 cups chicken broth, low sodium

1 (15.5-oz.) can cannellini beans, rinsed and drained (or 2 cups)

12 oz. brown rice penne pasta or elbows

¼ cup grated parmesan cheese

optional: fresh chopped parsley

1. Place ham, tomato sauce, garlic, pepper, and chicken broth in a large Dutch oven. Bring to a boil. Simmer covered 1 hour. Remove ham bone, allow to cool, and then remove meat from bone and chop into bite-size pieces. Discard bone and place meat back into Dutch oven.

2. In a separate pot, cook pasta in boiling salted water until al dente or not quite done (it will finish cooking to tender in Dutch oven). Drain pasta and place into Dutch oven with ham. (If desired, cut penne into smaller pieces). Add beans and cook uncovered 30 minutes on a low simmer, until beans are tender. Sprinkle in cheese and top with fresh parsley, if desired, to serve.

makes 12 servings @ 1 cup per serving

nutritional information

Calories: 155 ◆ Fat: 3.8 g ◆ Sat. Fat: 1.4 g ◆ Cholesterol: 24 mg ◆ Sodium: 606 mg ◆ Carbs: 18.6 g ◆ Fiber: 2.7 g ◆ Sugars: 1.8 g ◆ Protein: 12.1 g

citrus kale salad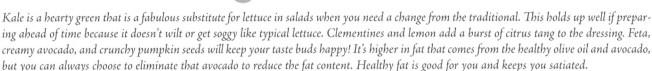

Kale is a hearty green that is a fabulous substitute for lettuce in salads when you need a change from the traditional. This holds up well if preparing ahead of time because it doesn't wilt or get soggy like typical lettuce. Clementines and lemon add a burst of citrus tang to the dressing. Feta, creamy avocado, and crunchy pumpkin seeds will keep your taste buds happy! It's higher in fat that comes from the healthy olive oil and avocado, but you can always choose to eliminate that avocado to reduce the fat content. Healthy fat is good for you and keeps you satiated.

4 cups coarsely chopped curly kale, ribs removed

2 clementines, segmented and pith removed

½ cup cherry tomatoes

½ avocado, sliced

½ cup crumbled feta cheese

2 Tbsp. pumpkin seeds

dressing

juice and zest of 1 lemon

juice and zest of 1 clementine

1 Tbsp. grated shallot

2 Tbsp. olive oil

½ tsp. salt

¼ tsp. pepper

1. Place kale in a large bowl. Toss with tomatoes, avocado, feta, and pumpkin seeds. In a small bowl whisk together dressing ingredients and toss into salad.

2. If making this in a mason jar, assemble as follows: place dressing on bottom, add kale, tomatoes, avocado, feta, and top with pumpkin seeds.

makes 2 servings

nutritional information

Calories: 454 ♦ Fat: 33.1 g ♦ Sat. Fat: 9.6 g ♦ Cholesterol: 34 mg ♦ Sodium: 1064 mg ♦ Carbs: 35.5 g ♦ Fiber: 9.4 g ♦ Sugars: 12.4 g ♦ Protein: 14.2 g

crustless spinach bacon quiche

Some staples I always have in my kitchen are eggs, bacon, and spinach. This way I know that even when my dinner plans get ruined by unexpected issues I can always throw together a quick quiche for my family. Making it without a crust releases me from the trouble of having a crust premade in the freezer. To me it's really not needed and my family loves it this way, so that's what I'm sticking with.

2 Tbsp. butter, room temperature

1 Tbsp. grated parmesan cheese

2 cups chopped fresh or frozen spinach

6 slices bacon, cooked crisp and chopped

1 cup shredded cheddar cheese

2 eggs

2 yolks

½ tsp. ground nutmeg

½ tsp. salt

¼ tsp. pepper

1. Preheat oven to 375 degrees. Grease a 9-inch skillet or cast iron pan with softened butter. Sprinkle grated parmesan cheese over butter.

2. Cook frozen or fresh spinach in the microwave, covered, for 2–3 minutes to wilt. Then squeeze as much juice out as possible. Spread into the pan. Sprinkle with bacon and cheese. In a bowl beat eggs and yolks together. Whisk in nutmeg, salt, and pepper. Pour over filling and bake for 35–40 minutes or until set.

makes 6 servings

nutritional information

Calories: 196 ◆ Fat: 16.2 g ◆ Sat. Fat: 7.4 g ◆ Cholesterol: 168 mg ◆ Sodium: 570 mg ◆ Carbs: .7 g ◆ Fiber: .2 g ◆ Sugars: .1 g ◆ Protein: 11.2 g

healthier fried rice

I'm sure you've seen how cauliflower can be substituted for potato, rice, and even flour pizza crust recipes. When I make mashed potatoes I never use a whole cauliflower head or my family will surely not eat it. Such is the same with this recipe for fried rice. I'd rather them not notice the cauliflower in the mix by making sure rice is also in there to keep them from asking what the heck they're eating. I'm happy to inform you that all the kids and the picky hubby didn't notice the cauliflower present, nor did they even ask what was different from the typical fried rice they know of.

3 cups grated raw cauliflower

1 cup diced onion

4 garlic cloves, minced

2 tsp. grated ginger

¼ cup sesame oil

1 cup diced carrots

1 cup frozen peas

4 eggs, beaten

3 cups cooked brown rice

optional: 2 Tbsp. rice vinegar or soy sauce or substitute (p. 125) with 1 tsp. salt and ½ tsp. pepper, any cooked protein, chopped scallions

1. Microwave cauliflower in a covered microwavable container for 3–4 minutes. Set aside.

2. Sauté onion, garlic, and ginger in sesame oil over medium heat until onion is softened and translucent. Stir in carrots and peas. Pour in beaten eggs and continue to cook until eggs are scrambled.

3. Add brown rice and cauliflower to egg mixture and stir to combine. Add rice vinegar or soy sauce and any cooked protein, if desired. Season with salt and pepper as needed, and top with scallions, if desired.

makes 9 servings

nutritional information

Calories: 190 ◆ Fat: 8.5 g ◆ Sat. Fat: 1.4 g ◆ Cholesterol: 80 mg ◆ Sodium: 342 mg ◆ Carbs: 21.9 g ◆ Fiber: 3.3 g ◆ Sugars: 3.1 g ◆ Protein: 6.3 g

fresh chicken spring rolls

This is a tasty egg roll–inspired filling, not fried, but instead used in a fresh brown rice spring roll wrapper. Satisfies that craving for egg rolls, only in a healthier way! If using regular soy sauce, remove salt.

2 Tbsp. toasted sesame oil

4 tsp. minced garlic

1 tsp. grated ginger

4 cups shredded cabbage

1 cup grated carrots

2 cups cooked and shredded chicken breasts

3 Tbsp. arrowroot powder

2 Tbsp. brown rice vinegar

2 Tbsp. soy sauce substitute (p. 125) or low-sodium soy sauce

½ tsp. salt

½ tsp. pepper

¼ cup chopped green onion

12 brown rice wrappers

1. Heat sesame oil in a large skillet over medium heat. Add garlic and ginger and cook until fragrant. Add in cabbage and carrots and cook until softened and tender. Stir in chicken.

2. In a small bowl whisk arrowroot, vinegar, soy sauce substitute or low-sodium soy sauce, salt, and pepper. Stir mixture into cabbage and chicken and heat through. Sprinkle in green onions. Cover and set filling aside.

3. Fill a shallow bowl with warm water. Place one brown rice wrapper at a time into water until softened. Flip over if needed. Carefully remove wrapper and place onto a clean cloth towel. Add filling to center of wrapper and roll up sides and then ends. Continue with remaining wrappers and enjoy immediately.

makes 6 servings @ 2 rolls per serving

* nutritional information

* Calories: 232 • Fat: 5.8 g • Sat. Fat: .7 g • Cholesterol:
40 mg • Sodium: 538 mg • Carbs: 25.8 g • Fiber: 3 g •
Sugars: 3.1 g • Protein: 19.8 g

light bites, salads, sides, and more   53

mock tater tots

My idea for these little tots was to try and replace packaged potato puffs. While the kids thought these looked awesome and certainly tried them, they did notice the taste wasn't potato. But, the point is they ate cauliflower anyway, and making it look like a potato puff made them try them. I love them for the fact they are low carbohydrate and I don't feel guilty at all in eating them. I'm sure you could substitute the cauliflower for homemade mashed potato and make homemade potato puffs for the family as well.

1 head cauliflower, washed, dried, and chopped (about 4 cups)

1 cup grated Parmesan cheese

¼ cup potato flour

1 egg

1 tsp. onion powder

1 tsp. garlic salt

1. Steam cauliflower for 20 minutes or until tender. Preheat oven to 450 degrees. Place cauliflower in a food processor and pulse until smooth.

2. Add remaining ingredients to cauliflower and mix together in a bowl. Form mixture into 40 cylinder-shaped tots and place on a cooling rack over a baking sheet. Bake for 25 minutes or until golden brown.

makes 8 servings @ 6 tots per serving

nutritional information

Calories: 56 ♦ Fat: 2 g ♦ Cholesterol: 27 mg ♦ Sodium: 345 mg ♦ Carbohydrates: 6.1 g ♦ Fiber: 1.3 g ♦ Sugars: 1.4 g ♦ Protein: 4 g

wild rice stuffing with bacon and brussels sprouts

If you're having company and you want something a little fancier for a side, this is the side dish to make. You've got some veggies, a nice salty bite with the bacon, and it really complements any entrée. I've made this for holidays a few times with rave reviews. I used 2½ cups of a brown wild rice medley I found, but if you can't find it combined like that just use a mix of both as the recipe suggests.

8 slices bacon, chopped

4½ cups chicken broth, low sodium

5 cups water

1¼ cups short brown rice

1¼ cups wild rice

8 oz. mushrooms, sliced

½ tsp. salt

½ tsp. pepper

16 oz. brussels sprouts, trimmed and thinly sliced

1. Cook bacon until crisp and drain on paper towels. In a large pot bring broth and water to a boil over medium heat. Add rice, cover, and simmer until tender, about 30 minutes. Turn off heat and let stand 10 minutes without removing the cover. Fluff with a fork.

2. In the same skillet used to cook bacon add mushrooms, salt, and pepper and cook until softened. Add brussels sprouts and cook for 5 minutes. Mix in rice mixture.

makes 10 servings @ 1 cup per serving

nutritional information

Calories: 212 ◆ Fat: 3.5 g ◆ Sat. Fat: .9 g ◆ Cholesterol: 7 mg ◆ Sodium: 302 mg ◆ Carbs: 36.4 g ◆ Fiber: 3 g ◆ Sugars: 1 g ◆ Protein: 9.1 g

mini zucchini cheese bites

I remember the first time I made these bites, the picky teen ate 3 before he asked what the green stuff in them was. He said, "Mom! I can't believe you got me to eat zucchini!" He then proceeded to eat 3 more!

2 cups shredded zucchini

½ cup grated parmesan

1 egg

¼ tsp. salt

⅛ tsp. pepper

¼ cup fresh chopped cilantro

1. Preheat oven to 400 degrees. Combine all ingredients together in a bowl. Grease a mini muffin tin or spray with nonstick cooking spray. Spoon mixture into 18 mini muffin cups. Bake 15 minutes or until golden brown. Enjoy with Mayo-Free Ranch Dressing (p. 118).

makes 4 servings @ 3 cheese bites per serving

nutritional information

Calories: 97 • Fat: 5.3 g • Sat. Fat: 2.7 g • Cholesterol: 72 mg • Sodium: 235 mg • Carbs: 4.3 g • Fiber: 1.2 g • Sugars: 2.1 g • Protein: 8.6 g

sweet potato pancakes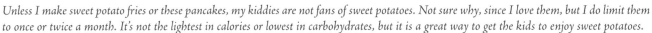

Unless I make sweet potato fries or these pancakes, my kiddies are not fans of sweet potatoes. Not sure why, since I love them, but I do limit them to once or twice a month. It's not the lightest in calories or lowest in carbohydrates, but it is a great way to get the kids to enjoy sweet potatoes.

3¼ cups cooked mashed sweet potatoes (about 2 sweet potatoes, 1½ lb. total)

2 Tbsp. butter

½ tsp. ground cinnamon

1 tsp. salt

½ tsp. pure stevia extract

1 tsp. maple extract

2 eggs

¼ cup brown rice flour or other gluten-free flour

¼ cup chopped chives

2 Tbsp. butter or oil (for pan frying)

optional: sour cream and chives

1. If sweet potatoes are not cooked yet, bake at 375 degrees for an hour until fork tender or microwave until cooked. Slice sweet potatoes in half and scoop out flesh into a bowl. Discard skin. Mix in butter and mash sweet potatoes well.

2. Stir in remaining ingredients until combined. Use a cookie scoop to measure out batter and then flatten into mini oval pancakes. Batter should make 16–18 mini pancakes.

3. Heat butter or oil in a large skillet and cook pancakes on both sides 3–5 minutes, or until golden brown. Remove with a slotted spoon and drain on paper towels. Enjoy immediately with optional toppings if desired.

makes 6 servings @ 3 mini pancakes per serving

nutritional information

Calories: 249 ◆ Fat: 9.4 g ◆ Sat. Fat: 4.2 g ◆ Cholesterol: 80 mg ◆ Sodium: 511 mg ◆ Carbs: 36.7 g ◆ Fiber: 4.8 g ◆ Sugars: 10.2 g ◆ Protein: 5.1 g

smoked salmon salad

It may be an acquired taste, but if you've never tried smoked salmon you will love it in this creamy-style salad. You can also replace the smoked salmon with tuna.

8 oz. skinless smoked salmon, flaked

¼ cup fresh chopped chives

½ cup Greek yogurt, plain, 2%

juice of 2 lemons

zest of 1 lemon

1 tsp. coarsely chopped capers

1 garlic clove, grated

½ red onion, chopped

½ tsp. salt

¼ tsp. pepper

1. Combine all ingredients in a bowl and mix well. Serve on a bed of lettuce.

makes 4 servings @ ½ cup per serving.

nutritional information

Calories: 150 ♦ Fat: 6.6 g ♦ Sat. Fat: 1.4 g ♦ Cholesterol: 52 mg ♦ Sodium: 466 mg ♦ Carbs: 3.2 g ♦ Fiber: .3 g ♦ Sugars: 2 g ♦ Protein: 18 g

shrimp cobb salad

Make once, eat twice. That's the motto with this recipe. I love a hearty salad but hate making one every day. I make this and I can have it the next day for lunch as well. Make it more convenient for traveling by assembling it in a mason jar.

½ cup Mayo-Free Ranch Dressing (p. 118)

1 cup cherry tomatoes

2 hard boiled eggs, chopped

½ avocado

6 oz. cooked shrimp, tails removed

1 lime

4 cups chopped romaine lettuce

4 slices turkey bacon, cooked crisp

1. Mason jar assembly: Add ¼ cup dressing to the bottom of each jar. Add ½ cup of tomato and then 1 egg, ¼ avocado, and 3 ounces of shrimp to each jar. Squirt some lime juice over shrimp and then add 2 cups of lettuce and top each jar with 2 slices crisp bacon, crumbled.

makes 2 servings

nutritional information

Calories: 424 ◆ Fat: 22.2 g ◆ Sat. Fat: 6.3 g ◆ Cholesterol: 398 mg ◆ Sodium: 880 mg ◆ Carbs: 19.2 g ◆ Fiber: 8.8 g ◆ Sugars: 7.7 g ◆ Protein: 42.5 g

baked garlic parmesan french fries

Kids always want fries and even I want fries on occasion. It's hard to resist eating more than one serving, but if you're going to have fries, these are better for you than buying frozen french fries or ordering them out somewhere. For one, these are baked not fried and so much tastier too! We keep the skin on them because they taste better that way, and the skins keep them crisp. The skin has all the nutrients and it's less work to make them, no peeling!

4 medium baking potatoes (about 4 cups when chopped)

2 Tbsp. olive oil or your choice

1 Tbsp. minced garlic

1 tsp. garlic salt

1 tsp. garlic powder

1 tsp. Italian seasoning

2 Tbsp. grated parmesan cheese

optional: 1 Tbsp. fresh chopped parsley

salt to taste

1. Preheat oven to 450 degrees. Scrub potatoes clean and pat dry. Cut potatoes into ¼-inch thick matchsticks.

2. In a large bowl, toss together potatoes, oil, garlic, and remaining seasonings except parmesan and parsley. Coat a baking sheet with cooking spray and spread potatoes on in a single layer. You may need 2 baking sheets so you don't overlap fries. Cook for 30–35 minutes or until golden and crispy. While still hot toss them with parmesan cheese and chopped parsley and salt if needed.

makes 8 servings @ ½ cup per serving

nutritional information

Calories: 91 ◆ Fat: 3.9 g ◆ Sat. Fat: .7 g ◆ Cholesterol: 1 mg ◆ Sodium: 139 mg ◆ Carbs: 13.8 g ◆ Fiber: 1 g ◆ Sugars: 1 g ◆ Protein: 2 g

garlic parmesan roasted chickpeas

The first time I made these I made a sweetened version for my kids, which is on the blog, and while they loved those they prefer this version. It's a fantastic way to provide a crunchy, nut-free snack for my boys with nut allergies. I've been making it for years and was lucky enough to have it featured in the Clean Eating Magazine Jan/Feb issue of 2012. You might want to double this recipe, since they never last more than a day in my house!

2 (15.5-oz.) cans chickpeas, rinsed and drained

2 Tbsp. coconut oil, melted, divided

½ tsp. salt

1 tsp. minced garlic

½ cup grated parmesan cheese

optional: cayenne, curry

1. Lay drained chickpeas on a paper towel to dry for 30 minutes. Preheat oven to 400 degrees.

2. Place 1 tablespoon coconut oil in a bowl, add chickpeas, and toss. Add salt, garlic, and parmesan. Add cayenne and curry if desired. Stir to coat. On a baking sheet or Silpat, spread chickpeas out, not overlapping them. Drizzle 1 more tablespoon melted coconut oil over the chickpeas. Bake for 20 minutes, stir, and continue to bake and stir for up to an hour, until crispy.

makes 10 servings @ ¼ cup per serving

nutritional information

Calories: 155 ◆ Fat: 5 g ◆ Sat. Fat: 3.2 g ◆ Cholesterol: 4 mg ◆ Sodium: 464 mg ◆ Carbs: 21.9 g ◆ Fiber: 4.2 g ◆ Sugars: 0 g ◆ Protein: 6.3 g

salt and vinegar toasted almonds

I have a thing for salt and vinegar potato chips. If you're trying to forgo the chips but still crave those flavors, here's a healthier crunchy snack to try. If you can't find white balsamic vinegar you can certainly use regular balsamic vinegar, although there are more natural sugars in regular balsamic.

2 cups raw almonds

½ cup white balsamic vinegar

2 tsp. coarse sea salt

1. Sauté almonds in a dry skillet over medium heat until fragrant. Add vinegar and simmer, stirring constantly, until vinegar is absorbed by almonds, 2–3 minutes. Turn off heat and sprinkle sea salt over warm almonds. Allow to dry in pan. Store in an airtight container for up to 2 weeks.

makes 8 servings @ ¼ cup per serving

nutritional information

Calories: 175 ◆ Fat: 15 g ◆ Sat. Fat: 1 g ◆ Cholesterol: 0 mg ◆ Sodium: 569 mg ◆ Carbs: 8 g ◆ Fiber: 3.5 g ◆ Sugars: 3.5 g ◆ Protein: 6 g

main dishes

crock pot balsamic chicken with balsamic bacon string beans

This recipe was one that went viral pretty quickly. I think because it's such a simple recipe, and the fact it's for a slow cooker makes it work for busy families. This can be made with chicken breasts as well but I would add ½ cup chicken broth because breasts need more liquid to keep them from drying out. I have also made this with chicken thighs not on the bone, which is the recipe on my blog, and both need about the same cooking time.

2 tsp. dried basil

1 tsp. salt

2 tsp. garlic powder

1 tsp. pepper

2 tsp. dried minced onion

2 lb. bone-in chicken thighs, skin removed

½ cup balsamic vinegar

1. Mix seasonings in a bowl and rub them all over chicken thighs. Place in crock pot. Pour in vinegar and cover. Cook 4 hours on high or 6 hours on low.

makes 8 servings @ 4 oz. per serving

nutritional information

Calories: 132 • Fat: 4 g • Sat. Fat: 1 g • Cholesterol: 85 mg • Sodium: 132 mg • Carbs: 5.6 g • Fiber: .1 g • Sugars: 5.2 g • Protein: 20.1 g

balsamic bacon string beans

This side works really nicely with any entrée, but in particular with my Crock Pot Balsamic Chicken (p. 74). And with the bacon, the kids will eat the string beans and even ask for more.

6 slices nitrate-free, uncured turkey bacon, diced

⅓ cup diced red onion

16 oz. string beans, ends cut off and cut in half

2 Tbsp. olive oil

1 Tbsp. balsamic vinegar

¼ tsp. salt

⅛ tsp. pepper

1. Cook bacon until crisp and remove from pan. Add onion, green beans, and olive oil to pan and cook until onion is tender, about 12 minutes. Turn off heat and add vinegar, salt, and pepper. Top with bacon and serve.

makes 4 servings

nutritional information

Calories: 138 ✦ Fat: 9 g ✦ Sat. Fat: .9 g ✦ Cholesterol: 38 mg ✦ Sodium: 446 mg ✦ Carbs: 6.6 g ✦ Fiber: 2.2 g ✦ Sugars: 2.8 g ✦ Protein: 10.1 g

traditional italian bolognese sauce

This fabulous recipe is my mom's. The only difference is I use turkey Italian sausage instead of pork. Obviously, to have that true authentic flavor pork sausage is better, but both are delicious. I grew up having this sauce every single Sunday. Nothing at restaurants or from a jar could ever compare to this sauce. Thank you, Momma, for letting me share it!

1 Tbsp. extra-virgin olive oil

1 cup onion, chopped

3 cloves garlic, minced

1 lb. sweet Italian turkey sausage

2 (28-oz.) cans crushed tomatoes

1 cup water

2 tsp. dried fennel seed

2 tsp. dried basil

2 tsp. salt

2 tsp. pepper

2 tsp. dried parsley

optional: red pepper flakes

1. Heat oil and cook onion and garlic in a large Dutch oven until onion is translucent. Remove casing from sausage and cook in Dutch oven until browned.

2. Add crushed tomatoes, water, and seasonings. Bring everything to a boil. Reduce heat, cover, and simmer for one hour. If sauce is too thick, add more water. If it's too thin for your liking, add some tomato paste. Keep refrigerated or freeze in an airtight container. Serve over pasta.

makes 20 servings @ ½ cup per serving

nutritional information

Calories: 71 • Fat: 2.8 g • Sat. Fat: .6 g • Cholesterol: 13 mg • Sodium: 363 mg • Carbs: 6.8 g • Fiber: .3 g • Sugars: .4 g • Protein: 4.9 g

mediterranean chicken cutlets

On a vacation last summer with my family, we enjoyed a nice dinner at a turkey farm restaurant. I ordered a Mediterranean turkey cutlet. I fell in love with the topping and knew I had to come home and make a version with chicken, since we don't purchase turkey cutlets much. Either will work and I bet this would also be fabulous over fish!

12 oz. chicken breasts (3 3-oz. breasts)

salt and pepper to taste

2 Tbsp. coconut oil

1 cup cherry tomatoes, halved

½ cup feta cheese

¼ cup kalamata olives

½ cup diced red onion

1 cup diced cucumbers

1 Tbsp. scallions

1 Tbsp. fresh chopped parsley

2 Tbsp. extra-virgin olive oil

1 Tbsp. lemon juice

1. Split breasts in half lengthwise. Salt and pepper both sides of chicken breasts. Cook chicken breasts in coconut oil on medium-high heat in a skillet. Cook 5 minutes on both sides. Toss remaining ingredients together in a bowl and serve over cutlets.

makes 6 servings

nutritional information

Calories: 225 ◆ Fat: 16.8 g ◆ Sat. Fat: 8.9 g ◆ Cholesterol: 52 mg ◆ Sodium: 474 mg ◆ Carbs: 5.5 g ◆ Fiber: .6 g ◆ Sugars: 3.6 g ◆ Protein: 15.7 g

mayo-free creamy coleslaw

The flavor and creaminess of coleslaw is a tough subject among foodies. There are so many variations, but no matter what, I find many are really picky about their slaw. You could certainly make this with mayonnaise if you prefer, but that will increase your nutritional information. Honestly, if you've never tried it mayo-free you might like it even better. My picky hubby, who is a coleslaw connoisseur, loves this version better than any other he's ever tried.

4 cups shredded cabbage or packaged coleslaw

¼ cup extra-virgin olive oil

¼ cup apple cider vinegar

1 tsp. celery salt

2 Tbsp. sour cream

½ cup plain Greek yogurt, 2%

1. Place shredded cabbage in a large serving bowl. Mix dressing ingredients together in a small bowl and toss with cabbage. Refrigerate 30–60 minutes or overnight.

makes 8 cups @ 1 cup per serving

nutritional information

Calories: 78 • Fat: 7.9 g • Sat. Fat: 1.6 g • Cholesterol: 4 mg • Sodium: 288 mg • Carbs: 1.7 g • Fiber: 0 g • Sugars: 1.7 g • Protein: 1.6 g

crock pot pulled pork

By now you know I love my crock pot. It's a must-have in a busy family and it gets used once or twice a week in my house. This is a tasty recipe that everyone loves because it's never dry, so all the kids enjoy it, as does the picky hubby. Serve with Barbecue Sauce (p. 116) and you've got a winner!

¼ cup tomato paste

½ cup apple cider vinegar

2 Tbsp. erythritol or honey (nutritional information will change if honey is used)

2 cups chicken broth, low sodium

4 medium garlic cloves, minced

1 tsp. cinnamon

2 tsp. dried mustard

1 tsp. ground cumin

2 tsp. paprika

½–1 tsp. chili powder

2 tsp. salt

4 lb. boneless pork shoulder, trimmed of excess fat

optional: 1-2 cups Barbecue Sauce (p. 116)

1. Place tomato paste, vinegar, erythritol, broth, and garlic in the crock pot and stir to combine. In a small bowl mix dry spices together and rub spice mixture all over pork. Place pork into the crock pot, cover, and cook on high 8–10 hours.

2. Shred meat with 2 forks and return meat to crock pot until ready to serve. If desired, add barbecue sauce to entire mixture or add onto individual servings.

makes 8 servings

nutritional information

Calories: 366 ◆ Fat: 18.3 g ◆ Sat. Fat: 6.3 g ◆ Cholesterol: 154 mg ◆ Sodium: 749 mg ◆ Carbohydrates: 2.4 g ◆ Fiber: .6 g ◆ Sugars: .8 g ◆ Protein: 45.1 g

baked parmesan-crusted fish sticks

I don't know about your kids but mine will eat anything when they can pick it up and dip it in sauce! I'm fortunate that my kiddies do love fish any way it's served. But rather than buying prepackaged fish sticks coated in bread crumbs from white flour, it's just as easy to make them at home and freeze them for an easy weeknight meal. Any flour you prefer will also work here. This is a winning recipe with the whole family!

2 lb. haddock or cod

¾ cup gluten-free flour

2 Tbsp. flaxseed meal

½ tsp. salt

¼ tsp. pepper

3 eggs

1¼ cup grated parmesan cheese

2 tsp. fresh chopped parsley

2 tsp. oil

1. Preheat oven to 450 degrees. Rinse fish and pat dry. Cut fish into 24 strips.

2. Place flour in bowl and mix with flax, salt, and pepper. In a small bowl, beat eggs. In another bowl mix parmesan and parsley. Coat fish strips, a few at a time, first in flour, then in eggs, then in parmesan. Place fish sticks on a greased baking sheet. Drizzle oil over fish sticks and bake 10 minutes. Flip sticks over and bake another 10 minutes or until golden brown. Serve with Mayo-Free Tartar Sauce (p. 122). Allow fish sticks to cool prior to freezing. Reheat in toaster oven or microwave for a quick meal.

makes 6 servings @ 4 strips per serving

nutritional information

Calories: 316 ♦ Fat: 11.2 g ♦ Sat. Fat: 4 g ♦ Cholesterol: 191 mg ♦ Sodium: 583 mg ♦ Carbs: 13 g ♦ Fiber: 2.6 g ♦ Sugars: .7 g ♦ Protein: 40.4 g

rosemary citrus roasted chicken with roasted root vegetables 🅲 🆂🅵 🅳🅵

In the winter months, cooking a whole chicken weekly is a much-loved family favorite. Adding some fresh citrus really gives the meat some nice flavor. Since I like really moist breast meat, I often roast the chicken upside down, meaning the breasts are on the bottom of the pan. It won't give you a crispy skin but since I often don't eat the skin anyway it doesn't matter to me. The directions below are for roasting the chicken the typical way, but you might be interested in trying it once to see which way you prefer. This is great for many leftover chicken recipes, like my Mayo-Free Chicken Salad Lettuce Wraps (p. 38) or a chicken soup! You can also roast the root vegetables at the same time as the chicken for a wonderfully balanced meal.

1 (6-lb.) whole chicken, neck and giblet discarded

1 tsp. salt, divided

½ tsp. pepper, divided

2 Tbsp. extra-virgin olive oil

2 oranges

2 lemons

2 garlic cloves, divided

3 sprigs fresh rosemary, divided

1. Preheat oven to 400 degrees. Pat chicken dry. Sprinkle cavity with ½ teaspoon salt and ¼ teaspoon pepper. Coat the skin with extra-virgin olive oil and then add remaining salt and pepper.

2. Juice oranges and lemons and set aside juice. Stuff juiced oranges, lemons, 1 garlic, and 2 sprigs of rosemary inside cavity. Add one garlic, chopped, to citrus juices and set aside.

3. Bake chicken in a 9 × 13 roasting pan for 1 hour. Then baste with garlic citrus juices. Chop remaining sprig of rosemary and sprinkle over chicken. Roast chicken 1 more hour, basting every so often until a thermometer inserted in inner thigh registers 170 degrees. Once out of the oven, cover with aluminum foil and let stand 10–15 minutes before carving.

makes 16 servings @ 6 oz. per serving

nutritional information

Calories: 332 • Fat: 24.3 g • Sat. Fat: 7 g • Cholesterol: 112 mg • Sodium: 446 mg • Carbs: .8 g • Fiber: 0 g • Sugars: .6 g • Protein: 28.5 g

roasted root vegetables

You've got to have delicious roasted veggies when making a roasted chicken, it's a must-have in my house. I try to make sure there's always at least one veggie in the mix that each child likes, especially if they aren't fond of some of the others in there. At least I know they'll eat one of them!

2 Tbsp. olive oil

1 lb. mixed potatoes (red, white, and purple)

1 red onion, cut into wedges

8 oz. baby carrots

8 oz. parsnips, peeled and cut in 1-inch pieces

½ tsp. salt

½ tsp. pepper

½ tsp. garlic powder

2 cups chicken broth, low sodium

1 Tbsp. fresh chopped rosemary

1. Preheat oven to 400 degrees. Pour oil onto a shallow baking sheet. Halve or quarter larger potatoes and keep smaller potatoes whole. Toss all vegetables in oil on baking sheet. Sprinkle salt, pepper, and garlic powder over vegetables.

2. Roast vegetables 30 minutes. Then pour broth into baking sheet and stir. Bake another 20 minutes or until fork tender. Sprinkle with fresh rosemary to serve.

makes 6 servings

nutritional information

Calories: 142 ✦ Fat: 4.5 g ✦ Sat. Fat: .6 g ✦ Cholesterol: 0 mg ✦ Sodium: 240 mg ✦ Carbs: 23 g ✦ Fiber: 4 g ✦ Sugars: 5.9 g ✦ Protein: 3.8 g

asian beef stir-fry 🄫 🅝 🅓

Who doesn't love a take-out fake-out that's healthy, right? My family loves a good stir-fry and I love that it's quick and easy. Here's another example of my kids eating veggies, but I make sure I include at least one of what each likes. Serve over rice if you desire.

1¼ lb. top sirloin steak

12 oz. broccoli florets

8 oz. sugar snap peas

2 Tbsp. coconut oil

1 red pepper, sliced

8 oz. mushrooms, sliced

4 oz. bean sprouts

stir-fry sauce

½ cup Quick Ketchup (p. 115)

3 Tbsp. erythritol

2 Tbsp. rice vinegar or Soy-Free Soy Sauce Substitute (p. 125)

¼ cup milk

1 Tbsp. Worcestershire sauce

2 Tbsp. mustard

½ cup mint leaves

1 scallion, chopped

1. Place steak in the freezer for 15 minutes. Once out of the freezer, slice very thin.

2. Bring a pot of water to a boil and blanch broccoli and sugar snap peas for 2–3 minutes. Drain and set aside.

3. Heat coconut oil in a large skillet and stir-fry meat until caramelized. Add red pepper, stir-fry a few minutes, and then add all vegetables.

4. In a bowl stir together sauce ingredients and toss in stir-fry right before serving. Top with fresh chopped mint leaves and scallions.

makes 8 cups @ 1 cup per serving

nutritional information

Calories: 214 ◆ Fat: 11 g ◆ Sat. Fat: 5.9 g ◆ Cholesterol: 63 mg ◆ Sodium: 164 mg ◆ Carbs: 5.7 g ◆ Fiber: 1.2 g ◆ Sugars: 2.4 g ◆ Protein: 22.6 g

coconut-crusted chicken tenders with mayo-free cilantro lime dip

I don't know one child or adult that doesn't love a good chicken tender every once in awhile. My family would eat these every night if I made them. Even the little man who's not a coconut fan loves these tenders, especially with the Cilantro Lime Dip.

¼ cup coconut flour

½ tsp. salt

¼ tsp. pepper

3 egg whites

juice of ½ lime

½ cup unsweetened shredded coconut

1 Tbsp. fresh chopped cilantro

1 lb. chicken tenderloins

2 Tbsp. coconut oil

1. Whisk coconut flour with salt and pepper in a shallow bowl and set aside. Beat egg whites with lime juice until frothy.

2. Mix shredded coconut with fresh cilantro in a shallow bowl. Dredge tenders first in coconut flour mixture, then in egg whites, then in shredded coconut. Be sure to coat both sides. Continue until all tenders are coated.

3. Heat oil in a large skillet and cook tenders, 5 minutes on each side, until golden. Drain on paper towels.

makes 4 servings @ 4 oz. per serving

nutritional information

Calories: 282 • Fat: 15.4 g • Sat. Fat: 11.2 g • Cholesterol: 65 mg • Sodium: 342 mg • Carbs: 5.8 g • Fiber: 3 g • Sugars: .2 g • Protein: 30.1 g

mayo-free cilantro lime dip

A nice light dip and a change from ranch dressing!

1 cup plain Greek Yogurt, 2%

juice of 1 lime

½ tsp. garlic salt

¼ tsp. pure stevia extract or ½ tsp. lemon liquid stevia

1 Tbsp. fresh chopped cilantro *— dried cilantro*

1. Whisk all ingredients together in a small bowl. Keep refrigerated until ready to serve.

makes 8 servings @ 2 Tbsp. per serving

nutritional information

Calories: 22 ◆ Fat: .6 g ◆ Sat. Fat: .4 g ◆ Cholesterol: 2 mg ◆ Sodium: 132 mg ◆ Carbs:1.3 g ◆ Fiber: 0 g ◆ Sugars: 1.2 g ◆ Protein: 2.9 g

crock pot chicken cacciatore

Cacciatore is a staple in my Italian family. The recipe on my blog for cacciatore is for the pressure cooker. Since many readers don't own a pressure cooker I adapted it for the crock pot. To make this on the stove, brown the thighs in oil and garlic and then add the rest of the ingredients. Cover and simmer for 30 minutes or until cooked through. An easy weeknight meal!

1 cup sliced onion

1 red pepper, sliced

3 lb. chicken thighs, skinless, bone in

1 tsp. salt

½ tsp. pepper

1 tsp. Italian seasoning

½ tsp. dried celery seed

2 tsp. dried oregano

1 tsp. dried basil

2 (12-oz.) cans tomato paste

2 Tbsp. extra-virgin olive oil

½ cup red wine or marsala wine or chicken broth

2 garlic cloves, minced

optional: ½–1 tsp. red pepper flakes

1. Place onions and pepper slices in the bottom of the crock pot. Season thighs on both sides with salt and pepper.

2. Mix dried seasonings with tomato paste and coat chicken thighs. Place thighs on top of veggies.

3. Whisk oil, wine, and garlic together. Pour over chicken. Cook on high 3–4 hours or low 6–7 hours.

makes 8 servings @ 6 oz. per serving

nutritional information

Calories: 226 ♦ Fat: 9.6 g ♦ Sat. Fat: 2 g ♦ Cholesterol: 128 mg ♦ Sodium: 753 mg ♦ Carbs: 4.7 g ♦ Fiber: .6 g ♦ Sugars: 3.1 g ♦ Protein: 30.4 g

oat flour pizza dough

In a family with kids, a pizza night is bound to happen. It's inevitable. I've made a whole wheat crust pizza, which is on my blog, but once I started experimenting with oat flour and made this gluten-free version they loved it even more. Whole wheat tends to make a dense pizza crust, but here I find the combination of the oat flour and the sorghum really resembled a white flour crust pizza the best. This recipe's dough makes two pizza crusts so you can freeze one and thaw it when needed.

3 Tbsp. oil

2 tsp. pure stevia extract

2 tsp. coconut sugar

1 tsp. salt

1¼ cup hot water

1 (¼-oz.) packet yeast

2 cups oat flour

1 cup sorghum flour

2 tsp. baking powder

1 tsp. xanthan gum

1. In a small bowl whisk oil, stevia, coconut sugar, and salt together with hot water. Add yeast. Do not stir—let sit for 8–10 minutes or until bubbles form.

2. In a stand mixer bowl, combine flours, salt, baking powder, and xanthan gum. Make a well in center of dry ingredients. Pour wet mixture into dry ingredients and mix at setting 2 for 2–3 minutes. Once combined, change the beater to a dough hook, keep setting at 2, and let the machine go for about 10 minutes. Or knead by hand for 10 minutes.

3. Remove dough and place into a bowl that is greased or sprayed with nonstick cooking spray. Cover with a towel and let rise for at least ½ hour, but 1 hour is better. Once risen, knead by hand for a minute or so and then separate dough into two balls. Wrap one in plastic wrap and store in the refrigerator or freezer. Spread other dough ball by hand onto a baking sheet that is greased or sprayed with nonstick cooking spray. Or use a rolling pin and sprinkle ground flaxseeds on clean surface to roll out dough into a circle to use on a pizza stone.

4. Bake in a preheated oven at 400 degrees for 15 minutes. Then remove and add toppings of choice. Bake another 20 minutes or until bottom of crust is crisp. Nutritional information is for pizza dough only.

1 pizza crust makes 8 servings

nutritional information

Calories: 254 ♦ Fat: 8.3 g ♦ Sat. Fat: 1.2 g ♦ Cholesterol: 0 mg ♦ Sodium: 292 mg ♦ Carbs: 39.9 g ♦ Fiber: 3.3 g ♦ Sugars: 1.8 g ♦ Protein: 8 g

lightened-up crock pot chicken herb stroganoff

I'm always trying to change up the chicken dishes for my family since we eat chicken a lot. I often turn to my best friend the crock pot. With a few simple ingredients you've got a perfect dinner waiting for you when you get home. Serve over pasta or rice or mixed veggies.

4 boneless chicken breasts, cut into bite-size pieces (2½ lb.)

3 Tbsp. butter

½ cup gluten-free flour

2 cups chicken broth, low sodium

1 cup light sour cream

4 oz. cream cheese

8 oz. sliced mushrooms

homemade italian seasoning

1 tsp. garlic salt

½ tsp. thyme

1 tsp. basil

2 tsp. dried onion

1 tsp. dried parsley

½ tsp. pepper

1 tsp. dried oregano

½ tsp. celery salt

1. Place chicken and butter into crock pot. Whisk flour, broth, sour cream, and cream cheese together in a small bowl and set aside. In a separate bowl stir together Homemade Italian Seasoning ingredients. Sprinkle Italian seasoning over chicken. Then pour broth/cream cheese mixture over chicken too. Cook on low, 2½ hours. Add sliced mushrooms and cook for an additional ½ hour.

makes 10 servings @ 4 oz. chicken per serving

nutritional information

Calories: 223 ♦ Fat: 10.8 g ♦ Sat. Fat: 5.3 g ♦ Cholesterol: 91 mg ♦ Sodium: 435 mg ♦ Carbs: 7.3 g ♦ Fiber: .7 g ♦ Sugars: 2.3 g ♦ Protein: 26.7 g

barbecue bacon turkey burgers

Although I'm not much of a barbecue fan, my hubby is. To please him and the rest of my crew I knew I needed a homemade, sugar-free version of barbecue sauce since they could eat it nightly and never tire of it. These burgers were a way for me to get my man to still enjoy a turkey burger without feeling like he was sacrificing that beefy flavor he loves. I love beef and use it in my meatballs and meatloaf, but to keep a burger lighter, since I love cheese and toppings, I chose turkey. Of course you could choose to use ground beef, but I wanted to show my family that they wouldn't miss the beef when turkey burgers are decked out like this.

6 slices uncured, nitrate-free turkey bacon

½ Vidalia onion

1 garlic clove

1½ lb. ground turkey

½ cup Barbecue Sauce (p. 116)

2 Tbsp. olive oil, divided

toppings: cheddar cheese, red onion, barbecue sauce, tomato, pickles, butter lettuce

1. Cook bacon in a sauté pan until crisp. Set aside to cool and then break into pieces. In a bowl, grate onion and garlic. Add turkey, barbecue sauce, and bacon. Form into 8 patties.

2. Drizzle 1 tablespoon of oil on an indoor griddle pan or heat an outdoor grill. Cook 4 burgers, 5 minutes on each side. Cook remaining 4 burgers with remaining tablespoon of oil, repeating procedure. Enjoy with additional toppings in a bun or lettuce wrap! Nutritional information is for turkey patty only.

makes 8 servings

nutritional information

Calories: 244 ◆ Fat: 15.1 g ◆ Sat. Fat: 5.7 g ◆ Cholesterol: 82 mg ◆ Sodium: 347 mg ◆ Carbs: 3.7 g ◆ Fiber: .4 g ◆ Sugar: 1.2 g ◆ Protein: 22.2 g

salmon spinach bake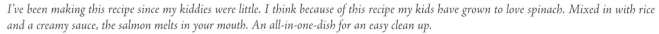

I've been making this recipe since my kiddies were little. I think because of this recipe my kids have grown to love spinach. Mixed in with rice and a creamy sauce, the salmon melts in your mouth. An all-in-one-dish for an easy clean up.

8 oz. fresh spinach

3 Tbsp. water

2 cups cooked brown rice

½ tsp. salt

¼ tsp. pepper

1 egg

½ cup sour cream, light

½ cup plain Greek yogurt, 2%

¼ cup plus 2 Tbsp. grated parmesan cheese

1 Tbsp. yellow mustard

1 Tbsp. lemon juice

2 Tbsp. milk, 1%

2 lb. salmon filets

1. Microwave spinach with water, covered, for 3 minutes. Drain, squeezing out as much water as possible.

2. Heat oven to 350 degrees. In a bowl combine rice, spinach, salt, and pepper. In another bowl whisk egg, sour cream, yogurt, parmesan, mustard, and lemon juice. Reserve ½ cup of sauce for topping on filets.

3. Add spinach/rice mixture to sauce in the bowl. Whisk milk into reserved sauce. Transfer rice/spinach mixture to a greased 1½-quart baking dish. Top rice with salmon filets. Drizzle remaining sauce over salmon filets. Top with additional parmesan cheese. Bake 30 minutes or until internal temperature registers 150 degrees.

makes 6 servings

nutritional information

Calories: 348 ♦ Fat: 13.2 g ♦ Sat. Fat: 3.3 g ♦ Cholesterol: 121 mg ♦ Sodium: 412 mg ♦ Carbs: 17.2 g ♦ Fiber: 1.4 g Sugars: 1.6 g ♦ Protein: 37.5 g

turkey taco stuffed peppers

Not one week goes by in our busy life without making tacos or quesadillas for the kids. I make this filling as a way to please everyone. Hubby and I enjoy the filling in peppers and the kids enjoy it in whole wheat tortilla wraps. I don't often add carbohydrates to this, but you could certainly add cooked brown rice or cooked quinoa to the filling. I would suggest just 1 cup of either.

3 sweet bell peppers, halved

1½ cups water

1 Tbsp. olive oil

1 cup chopped onion

1 clove garlic, minced

12 oz. ground turkey

½ tsp. salt

2 tsp. ground cumin

2 tsp. chili powder

1 cup canned or cooked black beans (if canned, rinse and drain)

1 cup salsa or homemade Enchilada Sauce (p. 121)

½ cup shredded cheddar cheese

1. Place pepper halves cut-side down into a 9 × 13 baking dish. Add ½ cup water. Cover and microwave 2 minutes or bake in an oven set at 350 degrees for 10 minutes or until softened slightly. Set aside.

2. Heat oven to 425 degrees. Heat oil in a skillet and cook onion and garlic until onion is translucent. Add turkey and seasonings and cook until turkey is no longer pink. Add black beans and salsa. Stir to combine.

3. Cook about 5 more minutes to heat beans through and then fill each pepper half with filling. Cover with aluminum foil and bake peppers for 30 minutes. Uncover, sprinkle with cheese and cook 5 minutes or until cheese is melted.

makes 6 servings

● **nutritional information**

Calories: 270 ◆ Fat: 12.6 g ◆ Sat. Fat: 4.9 g ◆ Cholesterol: 60 mg ◆ Sodium: 759 mg ◆ Carbs: 19.4 g ◆ Fiber: 4.5 g ◆ Sugars: 5.2 g ◆ Protein: 19.1 g

stuffed kale quinoa rolls

For a change of pace from lasagna or cabbage rolls, and since kale is my most beloved green, I created this recipe. Since the leaves vary in size after removing the stem, some will vary in how much stuffing you can fill into them. But for a Sunday supper meal that's low in carbohydrates, this recipe is a hit with my Italian family.

1 Tbsp. olive oil

12 oz. ground turkey (¾ lb.)

1 tsp. minced garlic

1 cup diced onion

½ tsp. salt

¼ tsp. pepper

¼ tsp. cayenne powder

½ tsp. nutmeg

18 large kale leaves, stems removed

1 cup water

½ cup uncooked dry quinoa

¾ cup ricotta cheese, part skim

2½ cups salsa, divided

1 egg, beaten

2 Tbsp. fresh chopped parsley

2 Tbsp. parmesan cheese

1. Heat oil in a large skillet and cook ground turkey, garlic, and onion until browned and onion is soft. Add salt, pepper, cayenne, and nutmeg.

2. Bring a large pot of water to a boil and blanch kale leaves for 2–3 minutes. Drain leaves and set aside. In a small pot on the stove, bring water and quinoa to a boil. Cover and reduce heat to a simmer. Cook quinoa for 12–15 minutes or until all water is absorbed. Fluff with a fork.

3. Add cooked quinoa, ricotta, 1 cup salsa, egg, and parsley to turkey mixture. Stir to combine. Fill kale leaves with turkey mixture in the center and roll up. Make 18 rolls. Preheat oven to 350 degrees. Place ½ cup salsa in a 9 × 13 baking dish and lay stuffed kale rolls seam-side down in the dish. Top rolls with 1 more cup of salsa. Cover and bake 30 minutes. Once out of the oven, sprinkle parmesan over rolls. Serve immediately.

makes 18 servings @ 1 roll per serving

nutritional information

Calories: 104 ♦ Fat: 4 g ♦ Sat. Fat: 1.4 g ♦ Cholesterol: 32 mg ♦ Sodium: 412 mg ♦ Carbs: 9.8 g ♦ Fiber: 1.9 g ♦ Sugars: 3.1 g ♦ Protein: 6.8 g

italian spinach meatloaf muffins

I was going to provide a typical meatloaf recipe because who doesn't love a good meatloaf recipe? We make it at least once a week. But since my family enjoys portioned bites of food, and since it certainly makes life easier when you need to pack a dinner and head to a game, these meatloaf muffins are just right for everyone. Hubby enjoys 2 while the kids have 1 each, and it works fabulously! You could also just make it in a regular loaf pan if you prefer.

2 eggs

¾ cup rolled oats

¼ cup plus 1 Tbsp. grated parmesan cheese, divided

1 tsp. salt

½ tsp. pepper

1½ cups homemade Quick Marinara Sauce (p. 108) or tomato sauce, divided

2 tsp. minced dried onion

2 cups fresh chopped spinach

1 cup sliced black olives

1 tsp. Italian seasoning

1½ lb. lean ground beef

optional: fresh chopped parsley

1. Preheat oven to 350 degrees. In a large bowl whisk eggs and stir in oats, ¼ cup parmesan, salt, pepper, 1 cup marinara sauce, onion, spinach, olives, and Italian seasoning. Mix in ground beef until combined.

2. Evenly divide mixture into a 12-capacity muffin tin. Top each individual meatloaf with remaining marinara sauce. Bake 30–40 minutes. Once out of the oven, sprinkle remaining tablespoon of parmesan cheese over each meatloaf muffin. Sprinkle with fresh parsley if desired. If baking as a whole loaf, cook time will be 45–60 minutes.

makes 12 muffins @ 1 muffin per serving

nutritional information

Calories: 130 ◆ Fat: 6.2 g ◆ Sat. Fat: 2.5 g ◆ Cholesterol: 53 mg ◆ Sodium: 450 mg ◆ Carbs: 7.2 g ◆ Fiber: .6 g ◆ Sugars: .2 g ◆ Protein: 11.1 g

crock pot shredded chicken fajitas

This recipe is a monthly meal in our home. You can do so many things with shredded chicken: make soft tacos, use as a topping for pizzas, or use in place of turkey in my Easy Turkey Enchilada Bake recipe (p. 110)! It's not spicy, but of course you can add more spice as you like.

1 onion, thinly sliced

1 red pepper, thinly sliced

1 green pepper, thinly sliced

2 tsp. chili powder

1 tsp. cumin

½ tsp. salt

¼ tsp. cayenne powder

3 lb. boneless, skinless chicken breasts

1 cup salsa

juice of 1 lime

optional: shredded cheese, sour cream, avocado, lettuce, tortillas

1. Place onion and peppers on the bottom of a greased crock pot. In a small bowl mix seasonings together and rub them over chicken breasts. Place chicken breasts on top of peppers and onion.

2. Top chicken with salsa and juice of 1 lime. Cook on high 4 hours. Shred chicken with 2 forks and place back into crock pot and stir veggies and chicken with salsa.

3. To serve with tortillas, place shredded chicken in middle of tortilla and add optional toppings if desired. Nutritional information is for chicken mixture only.

makes 20 servings @ ½ cup per serving

nutritional information

Calories: 72 ◆ Fat: .9 g ◆ Sat. Fat: 0 g ◆ Cholesterol: 36 mg ◆ Sodium: 301 mg ◆ Carbs: 2.7 g ◆ Fiber: .7 g ◆ Sugars: 1.5 g ◆ Protein: 14.2 g

mini italian stuffed meatballs with quick marinara sauce 🔵 🟢

We are Italian, so meatballs are much loved in our home. I try to change them up often so it doesn't get boring. Making mini stuffed meatballs with cheese like these ones are the perfect size for my kids to enjoy with Quick Marinara Sauce or homemade Quick Ketchup (p. 115), or for a host to serve as a little appetizer for a party, or even for moms to throw in a thermos for school lunches. You can also change the ground beef to ground turkey if you prefer. This is a winning recipe in my house; even the picky ones approve.

½ cup milk

½ cup grated parmesan cheese

½ cup rolled oats

2 Tbsp. Italian seasoning

1 tsp. minced garlic

½ tsp. salt

½ tsp. pepper

1½ lb. 95% lean ground beef

2 oz. cubed mozzarella (26 pieces)

1. In a small bowl combine milk, parmesan, and oats and set aside. In a large bowl stir together Italian seasoning, minced garlic, salt, and pepper. Add parmesan and oat mixture. Stir until incorporated. Add beef and mix until just combined. Make 26 mini meatballs.

2. Insert 1 small piece of mozzarella cheese into each meatball. Preheat oven to 350 degrees. Bake meatballs on a wire rack on top of a baking sheet for 15 minutes or until cheese is oozing out of meatballs slightly. Serve with Quick Marinara Sauce.

makes 6 servings @ 4 meatballs per serving

nutritional information

Calories: 294 ◆ Fat: 10.9 g ◆ Sat. Fat: 5.7 g ◆ Cholesterol: 106 mg ◆ Sodium: 434 mg ◆ Carbs: 7 g ◆ Fiber: .8 g ◆ Sugars: .3 mg ◆ Protein: 41.5 g

quick marinara sauce

This marinara sauce is a quick version that takes around 30 minutes. It's perfect with pasta, and it's great as a dip served with my Mini Italian Stuffed Meatballs!

1 Tbsp. extra-virgin olive oil

3 cloves garlic, minced

2 (28-oz.) cans crushed tomatoes

1½ cup water

2 tsp. dried basil

2 tsp. dried fennel seed

2 tsp. dried parsley

2 tsp. salt

pepper to taste

red chili pepper flakes to taste

optional: top with fresh chopped basil and grated parmesan cheese

1. Heat oil in a large pot or Dutch oven. Sauté garlic in oil. Add all other ingredients to the pot and bring to a boil. Once at a boil, cover and reduce heat. Simmer for 25–30 minutes. Add optional toppings and serve with meatballs or over your favorite pasta!

makes 10 servings @ ½ cup per serving

nutritional information

Calories: 69 ◆ Fat: 1.4 g ◆ Sat. Fat: .2 g ◆ Cholesterol: 0 mg ◆ Sodium: 465 mg ◆ Carbs: 11.5 g ◆ Fiber: 0 g ◆ Sugars: 0 g ◆ Protein: 2.8 g

easy turkey enchilada bake

Weeknights can be super difficult with soccer, scouts, dance, softball, karate, and 3 kiddies. I love this recipe and have been making it for years with slight variations each time. This one, I believe, is the best. It freezes well, so I often make two and freeze one. It's also an easy recipe to bring to friends or to families after they've had a new baby. I often hear from my friends that the whole family enjoyed it, and hearing that always puts on a smile on my face.

1 Tbsp. oil

1 tsp. minced garlic

1 cup diced onion

1 lb. lean ground turkey

½ tsp. salt

¼ tsp. pepper

1 cup mild salsa

6 corn tortillas

1 (10-oz.) can enchilada sauce or 1 cup home-made Enchilada Sauce (p. 121)

2 cups shredded cheddar cheese, divided

optional: additional ½ cup shredded cheese

toppings: scallions, sour cream, cilantro

1. Preheat oven to 350 degrees. In a large skillet heat oil and add garlic, onion, and turkey. Cook until turkey is browned and cooked through. Season with salt and pepper and pour in salsa. Stir to combine and set aside.

2. Place 2 tortillas in a 9 × 13 baking dish. Lay ½ of meat mixture onto tortillas and top with 1 cup cheddar cheese. Lay 2 more corn tortillas and then spread remaining meat mixture on top, along with remaining cheese. Top with remaining 2 tortillas. Pour enchilada sauce over last 2 tortillas and cover with aluminum foil.

3. Bake for 20 minutes and uncover. Add more cheese if desired. Bake 10 more minutes to melt cheese if needed.

makes 6 servings

nutritional information

Calories: 296 ◆ Fat: 15.4 g ◆ Sat. Fat: 5.3 g ◆ Cholesterol: 73 mg ◆ Sodium: 823 mg ◆ Carbs: 20.1 g ◆ Fiber: 2 g ◆ Sugars: 3.6 g ◆ Protein: 21.1 g

greek veggie burgers

On the weekends the hubby likes to have burgers. And as much as I like burgers, I also like to go with vegetarian burgers like this on occasion. I can make this recipe and enjoy it all week for lunch.

1 (15-oz.) can cooked chickpeas, rinsed and drained (1½ cups)

2 eggs

½ cup chopped onion

½ cup canned roasted red peppers, drained

1 cup fresh spinach

1 clove garlic, minced

1 tsp. dried oregano

1 tsp. dried dill

½ tsp. salt

¼ tsp. pepper

1 cup gluten-free bread crumbs

½ cup crumbled feta cheese

2 Tbsp. butter or oil

1. In a food processor, process chickpeas, eggs, onion, peppers, spinach, and garlic. Add seasonings and blend again. Transfer to a bowl and stir in bread crumbs and feta cheese. Form into 6 patties and refrigerate 15–20 minutes.

2. In a large skillet heat butter at medium heat and cook patties 2–3 minutes on each side. Serve with Tzatziki Sauce (p. 129) and with or without buns. Nutritional information is only for burger patties.

makes 6 servings

nutritional information

Calories: 292 ♦ Fat: 12.1 g ♦ Sat. Fat: 6 g ♦ Cholesterol: 90 mg ♦ Sodium: 811 mg ♦ Carbs: 35 g ♦ Fiber: 4.7 g ♦ Sugars: 2 g ♦ Protein: 9.4 g

condiments

quick ketchup

This is the easiest sugar-free ketchup recipe you will find—full of flavor and spot on with typical store-bought ketchup, but without the high fructose corn syrup. My little man loves it so much he warns me religiously when we are getting low on our ketchup so that we never run out.

¼ cup apple cider vinegar

¼ cup red wine vinegar

1 Tbsp. onion powder

1–2 Tbsp. powdered stevia

1 tsp. salt

1 Tbsp. olive oil

2 garlic cloves, minced

1 (28-oz.) can tomato puree

1 (12-oz.) can tomato paste

¼ tsp. ground cloves

¼ tsp. oregano

1. Whisk together apple cider vinegar, red wine vinegar, onion powder, 1 tablespoon powdered stevia, and salt. Pour into blender.

2. Pour oil, garlic, tomato puree, and tomato paste into blender. Blend until smooth. Add ground cloves and ¼ teaspoon oregano, and blend again. Taste and adjust stevia if needed. Refrigerate for up to two weeks.

makes 42 servings @ 2 Tbsp. per serving

nutritional information

Calories: 19 • Fat: .3 g • Cholesterol: 0 mg • Sodium: 61 mg • Carbohydrates: 3.6 g • Fiber: .3 g • Sugars: 1 g • Protein: .6 g

barbecue sauce

There's no way to go around it, for barbecue sauce you need to make homemade Quick Ketchup (p. 115), but since that recipe is so easy in the blender, this recipe is easy too. I often prepare both at the same time to have in the fridge whenever the family wants it.

½ cup water

2 Tbsp. erythritol or powdered stevia (not extract)

1 cup homemade Quick Ketchup (p. 115)

1 Tbsp. dried minced onion

¼ cup apple cider vinegar

1 Tbsp. all natural Worcestershire sauce

¼ tsp. cumin

¼ tsp. celery seed

¼ tsp. salt

1 tsp. natural maple extract

¼ tsp. ground cinnamon

1 Tbsp. unsweetened cocoa powder

optional: 2-3 dashes hot sauce

1. Whisk water and powdered stevia or erythritol altogether first, and then combine with remaining ingredients. Pour all ingredients into a saucepan, mix well, and bring to a boil. Reduce and simmer uncovered for 15 minutes or until mixture reduces and thickens.

makes 10 servings @ 2 Tbsp. per serving

nutritional information

Calories: 18 ◆ Fat: .3 g ◆ Sat. Fat: .1 g ◆ Cholesterol: 0 mg ◆ Sodium: 182 mg ◆ Carbs: 4.1 g ◆ Fiber: .4 g ◆ Sugar: .9 g ◆ Protein: .6 g

mayo-free ranch dressing

Many people are picky about ranch dressing, and capturing that authentic flavor without mayo was a challenge, but this has been tried again and again with many sharing that it's the closest to ranch they've ever tasted.

1 cup full fat buttermilk

¼ cup plain Greek yogurt, 2%

1 tsp. garlic powder

¼ tsp. salt

½ cup sour cream

¼ tsp. pepper

¼ cup chopped flat leaf parsley

2 tsp. fresh chopped chives

2 tsp. lemon juice

1. Whisk all ingredients together in a bowl. Seal in an airtight container. Chill in refrigerator 1 hour. Lasts in refrigerator for up to 3 days.

makes 10 servings @ ¼ cup per serving

nutritional information

Calories: 81 ✦ Fat: 6 g ✦ Sat. Fat: 3.4 g ✦ Cholesterol: 20 mg ✦ Sodium: 127 mg ✦ Carbs: 2.9 g ✦ Fiber: 0 g ✦ Sugars: 2.1 g ✦ Protein: 3.5 g

enchilada sauce

If you've never made enchilada sauce at home, it's definitely worth it. You can avoid some of the ingredients that are in typical canned enchilada sauce and cater the seasonings to your family, kicking up the heat with some red pepper flakes or hot sauce or more chili powder. This recipe is mild in heat.

3 Tbsp. extra-virgin olive oil

3 Tbsp. gluten-free flour

3 tsp. chili powder

1 tsp. ground cumin

¼ tsp. dried oregano

½ tsp. garlic salt

¼ tsp. ground cinnamon

1 cup chicken broth or vegetable broth, low sodium

1 cup water

6 oz. tomato paste

1. In a skillet, heat oil over medium heat. Reduce heat to low, add flour, and stir to combine to make a roux. Stir constantly for 1–2 minutes and then add chili powder, cumin, oregano, garlic salt, and cinnamon. Stir to combine.

2. Slowly add in chicken broth, water, and tomato paste. Turn up stove to medium-high heat and bring to a boil. Cook 5–10 minutes or until thickened. Allow to cool, and then refrigerate for up to 2 weeks.

makes 16 servings @ 2 Tbsp. per serving

nutritional information

Calories: 41 ✦ Fat: 2.8 g ✦ Sat. Fat: .4 g ✦ Cholesterol: 0 mg ✦ Sodium: 47 mg ✦ Carbs: 4 g ✦ Fiber: .7 g ✦ Sugars: 1.6 g ✦ Protein: 1.1 g

mayo-free tartar sauce

This tartar sauce is fantastic, even if you're not a fan of Greek yogurt. Subbing mayonnaise is an option if you desire, but please note that it will increase the nutritional information you see here. I often use plain Greek yogurt since my oldest has a soy allergy and regular mayo often has soybean oil in it.

¾ cup plain Greek yogurt, full fat

1 Tbsp. extra-virgin olive oil

3 Tbsp. diced dill pickles

1 Tbsp. fresh chopped parsley

½ tsp. salt

¼ tsp. pepper

1 clove garlic, minced

1 Tbsp. lemon juice

1. Mix all ingredients together in a bowl and refrigerate. Serve with Baked Parmesan-Crusted Fish Sticks (p. 82).

makes 8 servings @ 2 Tbsp. per serving

nutritional information

Calories: 34 ♦ Fat: 3.1 g ♦ Sat. Fat: 1.1 g ♦ Cholesterol: 4 mg ♦ Sodium: 278 mg ♦ Carbs: 1.4 g ♦ Fiber: 0 g ♦ Sugars: .9 g ♦ Protein: .5 g

soy-free soy sauce substitute

My oldest has a soy allergy so using any soy sauce in a recipe is a big no no for us. Although not identical to soy sauce, it's pretty close and works perfectly in recipes to replace soy sauce.

2 cups beef broth, low sodium

2 Tbsp. balsamic vinegar

2 tsp. molasses

1 tsp. sesame oil

¼ tsp. garlic powder

⅛ tsp. pepper

1. Add all ingredients to a pan and whisk to combine. Boil gently over medium heat until liquid is reduced to 1 cup, stirring constantly. About 15 minutes. Store in refrigerator for 3–4 weeks.

makes 8 servings @ 2 Tbsp. per serving

nutritional information

Calories: 18 ♦ Fat: .6 g ♦ Sat. Fat: .1 g ♦ Cholesterol: 0 mg ♦ Sodium: 111 mg ♦ Carbs: 2.6 g ♦ Fiber: 0 g ♦ Sugars: 1.5 g ♦ Protein: .8 g

sweetened condensed milk

I've never found a sweetened condensed milk made without added sugar so making it at home was a must for this momma. There are so many uses for this homemade version. So extremely simple to make, this is wonderful in coffee and desserts!

1 (12-oz.) can evaporated milk

1½ cups instant nonfat dry powdered milk

1 tsp. vanilla extract

1 tsp. vanilla liquid stevia

1. Mix all ingredients in a blender and refrigerate to allow to thicken, 2–3 hours. Keeps well for up to 1 week. If it thickens too much to pour, warm mixture over low heat or in the microwave.

makes 18 ounces @ 1 oz. per serving

nutritional information

Calories: 58 • Fat: 1.3 g • Sat. Fat: .8 g • Cholesterol: 7 mg • Sodium: 67 mg • Carbs: 6.2 g • Fiber: 0 mg • Sugars: 5.8 g • Protein: 4.5 g

tzatziki sauce

My hubby is a huge fan of this sauce. He'll enjoy it on any sandwich and asks for it often. Topping my Greek veggies burgers with it, I thought he might actually try them, but without meat and even though they were topped with his favorite Tzatziki sauce, I couldn't get him to try one bite. Win some, lose some with a picky man. I say more Greek burgers for me for lunches all week.

3 cloves garlic, minced

2 Tbsp. extra-virgin olive oil

juice of ½ lemon

1 tsp. salt

½ tsp. pepper

1 Tbsp. fresh dill or 1 tsp. dried

2 cups plain Greek yogurt, 2%

1 cup sliced English cucumber, seeds removed

1. Place all ingredients together in a food processor and process until smooth. Cover and refrigerate 1 hour before serving.

makes 20 servings @ 2 Tbsp. per serving.

nutritional information

Calories: 28 ◆ Fat: 1.9 g ◆ Sat. Fat: .5 g ◆ Cholesterol: 4 mg ◆ Sodium: 128 mg ◆ Carbs: 1.7 g ◆ Fiber: 0 g ◆ Sugars: 1.4 g ◆ Protein: 2.2 g

beverages

fake-out fruit punch

You can certainly find juice in a health food store that doesn't contain added sugars. They may be quite expensive, but of course they are a better option that typical juice loaded with sugars. I don't often buy any juice, but I do occasionally purchase juice boxes for easy packing when going to the beach or for a friend's pool party. My daughter is not a fan of tea so when I make this I hide the tea bags brewing or she won't drink it. She actually thinks she doesn't like cold tea, but she loves this Fake-out Fruit Punch!

4 tea bags herbal flavored decaffeinated tea

4 cups boiling water

4 cups cold water

4 full droppers cherry liquid stevia

1. Place tea bags in a large mason jar. Pour boiling water into mason jar and allow tea to steep for 15 minutes. Remove tea bags and add cold water and stevia. Stir to combine and refrigerate.

makes 2 quarts

nutritional information

This is zero grams for all nutritional information categories.

cocoa mix

I believe every cookbook should have a homemade cocoa mix recipe. If you're going to reduce your sugar intake and you have kids in the house, this recipe is a must for those cold winter days of sledding and making snowmen.

2 cups unsweetened cocoa powder

2 tsp. arrowroot powder

1 tsp. salt

2 Tbsp. powdered stevia

1. Whisk ingredients together and store in an airtight container. To make 1 serving, add 2 tablespoons of cocoa mix to a mug and pour in 1 cup of hot milk. Whisk until combined and enjoy!

makes 16 servings @ 2 Tbsp. per serving

nutritional information

Calories: 23 ◆ Fat: 1 g ◆ Sat. Fat: 0 g ◆ Cholesterol: 0 mg ◆ Sodium: 145 mg ◆ Carbs: 6.9 g ◆ Fiber: 4 g ◆ Sugars: 0 g ◆ Protein: 1 g

vanilla coffee creamer

Since I'm such a coffee lover, there was no way I'd miss an opportunity to provide a coffee creamer for this cookbook. Unfortunately I'm also super picky in how I like my coffee. I want it creamy since I don't use sugar. I've tried using all almond milk, all coconut milk, just using evaporated milk, or half and half and full cream, but nothing made me happy with my coffee until I made this combination. This has the most perfect consistency. If you're not a fan of vanilla simply remove it and add your own extract of choice and/or stevia or another sweetener you like.

1 (12-oz.) can evaporated milk

1½ cups nonfat dry powdered milk

1½ cups unsweetened vanilla almond milk

2 tsp. vanilla extract

2 tsp. vanilla liquid stevia

1. Pour all ingredients into a mason jar, cover, and shake vigorously until combined well. Use the expiration dates on your milk or cream used in recipe as your guide to how long creamer will last. If you don't have vanilla stevia use 3 teaspoons of vanilla extract.

makes 40 servings @ 2 Tbsp. per serving

nutritional information

Calories: 27 ◆ Fat: .8 g ◆ Sat. Fat: .4 g ◆ Cholesterol: 3 mg ◆ Sodium: 34 mg ◆ Carbs: 2.8 g ◆ Fiber: 0 g ◆ Sugars: 1.6 g ◆ Protein: 2 g

mocha protein coffee frappe

I don't know about you, but this momma runs on coffee and loves chocolate, but I don't want to drink my calories for the day away. I wanted a double-duty-type frappe full of protein to serve as a quality snack in between meals, but that would also give me a little energy boost with some caffeine. If you don't have the cocoa mix made, just substitute unsweetened cocoa powder and increase your sweetener. You could certainly make this caffeine-free using decaf coffee if you prefer.

2 Tbsp. homemade Cocoa Mix (p. 134)

½ cup unsweetened almond milk

1 scoop unsweetened chocolate protein powder

¼ cup brewed coffee

1 tsp. vanilla extract

1 cup crushed ice

1. Blend all ingredients in a blender, taste, and adjust if needed with stevia.

makes 2 servings.

nutritional information

Calories: 80 ◆ Fat: 2.2 g ◆ Sat. Fat: .5 g ◆ Cholesterol: 32 mg ◆ Sodium: 143 mg ◆ Carbs: 5.3 g ◆ Fiber: 2.8 g ◆ Sugars: .5 g ◆ Protein: 12.3 g

lemonade

We make this lemonade 2–3 times a week throughout the year. No need to buy expensive juice or powdered sugary lemonade mix when you can make this at home. The kids love getting involved and juicing the lemons. Lemons are so healthy, with antibacterial properties, so I don't mind them drinking 2–3 glasses of this a day, knowing they aren't drinking sugar with it.

6 fresh lemons

2 quarts water

1 tsp. lemon liquid stevia

1 lemon to slice and add to pitcher

1 cup ice cubes

1. Slice lemons in half, squeeze out juice into a bowl, and remove seeds (about ½ cup juice all together). Add juice to a large pitcher. Add water to the pitcher. Stir in stevia. Taste it and decide if sweet enough. Cut 1 lemon into slices and add to pitcher. Add ice cubes and serve!

makes 8 servings @ 8 oz. per serving

nutritional information

Calories: 9 ◆ Fat: 0 g ◆ Sat. Fat: 0 g ◆ Cholesterol: 0 mg ◆ Sodium: 0 mg ◆ Carbs: 3 g ◆ Fiber: 0 g ◆ Sugars: 0 g ◆ Protein: 0 g

sweet treats

fudgy flourless chocolate brownies

Here's another recipe I was hesitant to make but my family now loves it and still has no idea beans are in them. First posted on my blog back in February 2013, I had no idea what a big hit they would be. I don't like to share that they are made with black beans because I think most people would be turned off to making them. But when you taste them, you'd never know, and since I've made this a million times for my family, friends, and Cub Scouts, no one has said anything other than they can't believe they are flourless and contain no added sugar.

If you can't find sugar-free chocolate chips sweetened with stevia I would recommend trying unsweetened carob chips that can be found in most health food stores in the bulk section. Carob is naturally sweet on its own with no other additives. Be careful when purchasing them, since there are also carob chips sweetened with beet sugar, but I find the unsweetened ones to be just fine to use.

1¼ cups sugar-free chocolate chips

1 (15.5-oz.) can black beans, rinsed and drained

¼ cup unsweetened carob powder or cocoa powder

2 eggs

1/3 cup olive oil or coconut oil, melted

¼ tsp. cinnamon

2 tsp. vanilla extract

¼ tsp. salt

½ tsp. baking powder

1 tsp. instant coffee

2 Tbsp. powdered stevia

optional: Chocolate Fudge Frosting (p. 193)

1. Preheat oven to 350 degrees. Line an 8 × 8 baking dish with parchment paper. Spray parchment paper with nonstick cooking spray. Process all ingredients in a food processor until smooth.

2. Pour batter onto the parchment paper in the baking dish and smooth out to the edges of the dish. Bake 30 minutes or until a toothpick comes out clean. Cool pan on wire rack for 10 minutes and then remove brownies by holding the edges of the parchment paper and lifting out. Transfer onto a wire rack to cool before frosting (if desired) and slicing on a cutting board.

makes 16 servings

nutritional information

Calories: 146 ♦ Fat: 10.4 g ♦ Sat. Fat: 4.1 g ♦ Cholesterol: 22 mg ♦ Sodium: 79 mg ♦ Fiber: 4.2 g ♦ Carbs: 16.3 g ♦ Sugars: 1.7 g ♦ Protein: 3.8 g

classic fudge 🐮

When you have a family that loves fudge as much as mine, I had to learn early on to make it for them sugar-free. I have a crock pot recipe for fudge on my blog, but this one is even quicker. The Sweetened Condensed Milk recipe takes no time at all and then you just melt the rest of the ingredients and refrigerate! If you can't find sugar-free chocolate chips I would recommend trying to find the highest cocoa percentage you can in a milk chocolate candy bar or chocolate chips. The family says this fudge is the best one I've ever made.

2½ cups sugar-free chocolate chips

1 recipe homemade Sweetened Condensed Milk (p. 127)

2 tsp. cinnamon

1 tsp. vanilla extract

3 Tbsp. butter

coarse sea salt

1. Line an 8 × 8 baking dish with parchment paper. Grease parchment or spray parchment with nonstick cooking spray. Melt chocolate chips in a glass bowl over simmering water in a saucepan.

2. Once chocolate chips are melted, add all ingredients except sea salt together and whisk until smooth. Pour into baking dish and sprinkle with sea salt. Refrigerate for 2 hours.

makes 24 servings

nutritional information

Calories: 149 ◆ Fat: 9.2 g ◆ Sat. Fat: 5.6 g ◆ Cholesterol: 9 mg ◆ Sodium: 60 mg ◆ Carbs: 18.1 g ◆ Fiber: 3.4 g ◆ Sugars: 4.4 g ◆ Protein: 5.1 g

chocolate macaroons

A delicious soft and chewy macaroon has always been a favorite cookie of my dad's. I'm not much of a cookie girl myself but there's just something about macaroons. This one hits the spot for a chocolate chewy craving.

4 egg whites

¼ tsp. salt

1 tsp. coconut liquid stevia or chocolate stevia or plain stevia

2 Tbsp. coconut milk, unsweetened

2¼ cups unsweetened shredded coconut

2½ oz. unsweetened baking chocolate

7 oz. coconut butter

2 tsp. powdered stevia or 6 packets

optional topping: ½ cup sugar-free chocolate chips melted with 2 Tbsp. butter, or butter substitute if needed for dairy-free, and a sprinkle of toasted shredded coconut

1. Preheat oven to 350 degrees. Whisk egg whites, salt, and stevia until frothy. Pour coconut milk into egg mixture. Pour shredded coconut into mixture and stir until moistened.

2. Melt baking chocolate and coconut butter in a small bowl, 30 seconds at a time in the microwave or over a double boiler. Stir until smooth and then add to coconut mixture.

3. Using a cookie scoop, make 21 rounded cookies and place on a parchment-lined baking sheet. Bake for 20–25 minutes. Cool 5 minutes and then transfer to a wire rack to complete cooling. Once cooled, add chocolate drizzle if desired. Nutritional information is without optional chocolate drizzle.

makes 21 cookies

nutritional information

Calories: 140 • Fat: 13.7 g • Sat. Fat: 10.1 g • Cholesterol: 0 mg • Sodium: 70 mg • Carbs: 4.3 g • Fiber: 2.6 g • Sugars: .8 g • Protein: 3 g

nut-free florentine lace cookies

Florentine lace cookies filled with chopped nuts are so delicate and lovely during the holidays. My youngest loves that I make these especially for him. Actually my entire family prefers these without nuts over the ones I make with nuts. If your family doesn't have nut allergies, simply replace the pumpkin and sunflower seeds with chopped nuts of choice.

1 cup raw pumpkin seeds

1 cup roasted, salted sunflower seeds

2 Tbsp. gluten-free flour

½ cup butter, room temperature (1 stick)

¾ cup Homemade Powdered Sugar Substitute (recipe below) or powdered erythritol

⅓ cup brown rice syrup

⅓ cup heavy cream

1. Preheat oven to 350 degrees. Stir seeds with flour and set aside. In a small saucepan melt butter, Homemade Powdered Sugar Substitute, brown rice syrup, and cream on medium-high heat until dissolved. Bring to a boil and turn off heat. Pour seed mixture into the pan and stir to coat well.

2. Cool 10 minutes and then drop by a tablespoon each onto a parchment-lined baking sheet. Bake 12–15 minutes or until golden brown. Slide the parchment with cookies onto a cooling rack for 60 minutes or until completely cool. Carefully wedge a thin spatula under cookies to remove from parchment and place onto paper towels to crisp up for another 2 hours.

makes 34 cookies.

nutritional information for 1 cookie

Calories: 83 ◆ Fat: 6.7 g ◆ Sat. Fat: 2.3 g ◆ Cholesterol: 9 mg ◆ Sodium: 26 mg ◆ Carbs: 4.3 g ◆ Fiber: .8 g ◆ Sugars: 1.8 g ◆ Protein: 1.3 g

homemade powdered sugar substitute

2 cups erythritol

2 Tbsp. arrowroot powder

1. Add to blender and blend on high until combined.

gram's butter balls

I never thought I'd be able to remake a sugar-free and gluten-free version of my grandmother's butter ball recipe. I honestly wasn't sure they'd even taste good. But again I was proven wrong. My mom even said these are just as good as gram's! What a huge compliment! I made a nut-free version so my little man could enjoy them and made another version including the pecans to share during the holidays with the family. Either option is equally delicious!

1 cup softened butter

2 Tbsp. plain Greek yogurt, full fat

1 cup erythritol, divided

1 tsp. vanilla extract

1 tsp. vanilla liquid stevia

2 cups gluten-free flour (I used my own blend)

¼ tsp. salt

optional: 1 cup chopped pecans

1. Preheat 400 degrees. In a stand mixer blend butter, yogurt and ½ cup erythritol. Place the other ½ cup of erythritol into a shallow bowl and set aside.

2. Once butter/yogurt mixture is combined, add vanilla extract and stevia. Slowly pour in flour and salt a little at a time. Stir in chopped pecans if using.

3. Shape into 1-inch balls. Place on a parchment-lined baking sheet. Bake 10 minutes. Once out of the oven and while still warm, roll butter balls in erythritol. Nutritional information is without pecans.

makes 18 servings @ 2 butter balls per serving

nutritional information

Calories: 167 ◆ Fat: 13.9 g ◆ Sat. Fat: 6.8 g ◆ Cholesterol: 27 mg ◆ Sodium: 34 mg ◆ Carbs: 10.7 g ◆ Fiber: 1.7 g ◆ Sugars: .5 g ◆ Protein: 1.9 g

chocolate chip oat cookies

When it comes to making cookies I find using erythritol in combination with stevia makes for the best texture in a gluten- and sugar-free cookie. These chocolate chip cookies have terrific flavor with a cross between an oatmeal cookie and a chocolate chip cookie.

1 cup quick oats, certified gluten-free

1½ cups gluten-free flour

1 tsp. xanthan gum

1 tsp. baking soda

½ tsp. ground cinnamon

½ tsp. salt

½ cup softened butter

1 cup erythritol

1 tsp. vanilla liquid stevia

1 tsp. vanilla extract

3 eggs

1 cup sugar-free chocolate chips or unsweetened carob chips

1. Preheat oven to 350 degrees. Whisk first 6 ingredients together in a bowl. Place butter, erythritol, stevia, extract, and eggs in a stand mixer and blend until incorporated.

2. Gradually pour dry ingredients into wet ingredients in the mixer and blend until batter is combined well. Stir in chocolate chips.

3. Use a small cookie scoop to place cookie dough on a parchment-lined baking sheet. Bake for 15 minutes. Let cool.

makes 32 cookies @ 2 cookies per serving

nutritional information

Calories: 180 • Fat: 11.3 g • Sat. Fat: 5.7 g • Cholesterol: 49 mg • Sodium: 125 mg • Carbs: 20.1 g • Fiber: 3.9 g • Sugars: .5 g • Protein: 4.2 g

chocolate tart

If you haven't figured out that I'm a chocolate lover, you will after this purely decadent pie recipe. Heavy, rich, smooth, and luscious with every silky bite, just a small slice is all you need to feel satisfied with this treat. It's a fantastic dessert to bring to a party with friends and easy to make ahead for any occasion. I love recipes that no one has any idea are sugar-free, and this is certainly one of the best pies I've made as of yet. Yes, it's high in calories and fat, but it's for special occasions, not a weeknight dessert. It is, however, high in fiber and protein, low in carbohydrates, and sugar-free, so you can still feel better about indulging.

1½ cups heavy cream

4 oz. unsweetened baking chocolate

1 tsp. vanilla extract

1 tsp. vanilla liquid stevia

2 Tbsp. powdered stevia or erythritol

½ tsp. salt

4 eggs

1 Nut-Free Tart Shell, prebaked

1. Heat heavy cream in a saucepan over medium-low heat until cream simmers around edges. Add chocolate and stir until melted.

2. Turn off heat and add vanilla, liquid stevia, powdered stevia, and salt. Set aside. Beat eggs in a stand mixer. Add some chocolate mixture to beaten eggs to temper them. Then pour remaining chocolate mixture into eggs and blend together until incorporated.

3. Pour into cooled tart shell. Bake in oven set at 325 degrees for 20 minutes or until filling is glossy. If you see bubbles or cracks, remove immediately and let cool. Then refrigerate.

makes 12 servings

nutritional information

Calories: 278 ♦ Fat: 25.3 g ♦ Sat. Fat: 9.5 g ♦ Cholesterol: 101 mg ♦ Sodium: 131 mg ♦ Carbs: 8.9 g ♦ Fiber: 5.3 g ♦ Sugars: .1 mg ♦ Protein: 10 g

nut-free tart shell

Finding alternative crusts or crust recipes that don't contain some form of a nut is practically impossible to find in stores and online. I knew if I wanted to make a pie for this cookbook, a good nut-free crust was a must-have. I personally prefer desserts without crust, but I know that doesn't work for all pie recipes. This chocolate tart crust could be used for many recipes, specifically for my chocolate tart recipe, but also for making little tartlets or a dessert pizza or any other creamy concoction you could think of. The sunflower seeds provide the best texture needed for a smooth dessert or cream pie.

1¾ cups raw, unsalted sunflower seeds

¼ cup unsweetened cocoa powder

1 egg

2 Tbsp. butter

1 Tbsp. powdered stevia or erythritol or ½ tsp. pure stevia extract

1. Process all ingredients into a food processer. Mold or form shell in a tart pan. Bake at 350 degrees for 10 minutes. Use as desired.

makes 12 servings

nutritional information

Calories: 155 ♦ Fat: 13.4 g ♦ Sat. Fat: 2.6 g ♦ Cholesterol: 20 g ♦ Sodium: 6 mg ♦ Fiber: 5.6 g ♦ Carbs: 3.7 g ♦ Sugar: 0 g ♦ Protein: 6.3 g

lemon pudding cakes   *(sub with dairy-free heavy cream)*

We buy lemons by the dozens, using them in homemade lemonade, smoothies, and savory dishes. But I don't have nearly enough lemony desserts, hence this recipe. Made into individual servings here, but this could easily be made into a pie dish for transporting to a friend's house. These simple ingredients make a luscious lemony pudding on the bottom and a soft, cake-like texture on the top. One recipe tester made this dairy-free by subbing the heavy cream with coconut cream. The recipe tester also added chopped carrots for a citrusy style carrot cake.

3 eggs, separated

2 Tbsp. gluten-free flour (I used sorghum)

2 Tbsp. lemon zest (about 4 lemons' worth)

¼ cup lemon juice (2–3 lemons' worth)

1 tsp. lemon liquid stevia

1 cup heavy cream

¼ tsp. salt

optional toppings: whipped cream and lemon zest

1. Preheat oven to 350 degrees. Whisk yolks in a bowl, and then stir in flour, lemon zest, lemon juice, stevia, and heavy cream. In a stand mixer beat egg whites and salt until soft peaks form.

2. In portions, fold egg whites into yolk mixture. Pour into 6 ramekins. Place ramekins in a large 9 × 13 baking dish. Pour 3 cups of hot water into baking dish and place in the oven in the center. Bake until light and fluffy, 25–30 minutes.

3. Remove from water bath and allow to cool 1 hour. Then refrigerate and chill 2 hours. Top with whipped cream and lemon zest if desired when ready to serve. Nutritional information is for pudding cake only.

makes 6 servings

nutritional information

Calories: 116 ◆ Fat: 9.4 g ◆ Sat. Fat: 5.1 g ◆ Cholesterol: 117 mg ◆ Sodium: 132 mg ◆ Carbs: 3.3 g ◆ Fiber: .3 g ◆ Sugars: .3 g ◆ Protein: 3.9 g

nut-free magic bars 🅝🅕

I'm sure you have heard of magic bars, right? Basically it's graham crackers crumbled and melted with butter as the crust and it's topped with sweetened condensed milk, chocolate chips, and chopped nuts. Shredded coconut is often added. It's very easy with store-bought items, but healthy? Not so much. This version is much healthier, is nut-free, and tastes fantastic. My kids absolutely love it! You could also use the Graham Cracker recipe (p. 175) and combine it with butter for your crust. You could also replace the toppings with whatever toppings you like.

1 (15.5-oz) can coconut milk

¼ cup coconut sugar

crust

1 cup sunflower seeds, raw

½ cup shredded coconut

¼ tsp. ground cinnamon

1 tsp. vanilla extract

1 tsp. pure stevia extract

¼ tsp. salt

¼ cup butter

toppings

1 cup sugar-free chocolate chips, divided

½ cup shredded coconut

1. Over low heat combine coconut milk and coconut sugar in a small saucepan and bring to a boil. Simmer uncovered for 30 minutes, stirring constantly until reduced and thick. Set aside.

2. Preheat oven to 350 degrees. For crust, first pour sunflower seeds into food processor and process until they resemble flour. Combine remaining crust ingredients with processed sunflower seeds until incorporated.

3. Line an 8 × 8 baking dish with parchment paper and grease or spray with nonstick cooking spray. Spread and press crust onto the parchment. Pour coconut milk mixture over crust. Top with ½ cup chocolate chips, then shredded coconut, and then remaining chocolate chips. Bake for 30 minutes. Let cool for 15 minutes. Then remove onto a cutting board to slice into 12 squares or refrigerate until ready to serve.

makes 12 servings

nutritional information

Calories: 283 ♦ Fat: 24 g ♦ Sat. Fat: 13.4 g ♦ Cholesterol: 10 mg ♦ Sodium: 90 mg ♦ Carbs: 18.2 g ♦ Fiber: 3.7 g ♦ Sugars: 5.3 g ♦ Protein: 3.1 g

chocolate mousse

This recipe is an adaption of the one on my blog, which is equally delicious but adds a banana. This one is still creamy even without the banana, and now lower in carbohydrates as well. For those of us who have dairy intolerances this is a quick and great alternative to milk-based pudding. I promise you the avocado flavor will not be anything you can notice; it's all about the chocolate here. You can substitute any milk of choice, but since this is for me, not the kids, I used almond milk. If for my boys with nut allergies, I would use dairy milk or even coconut milk.

1 avocado, pitted and peeled

¼ cup unsweetened cocoa powder

½ cup unsweetened almond milk

1 tsp. vanilla extract

⅛ tsp. salt

¼ tsp. liquid vanilla or chocolate stevia

1. Add all ingredients in a high powdered food processor or blender and blend until completely smooth.

makes 2 servings.

nutritional information

Calories: 145 ♦ Fat: 12.6 g ♦ Sat. Fat: 2.3 g ♦ Cholesterol: 0 mg ♦ Sodium: 204 mg ♦ Carbs: 11.9 g ♦ Fiber: 8.4 g ♦ Sugars: .4 g ♦ Protein: 3.7 g

apple cake *(sub with vegan butter)*

I never met an apple I didn't like. There's a whole wheat version of this apple cake on my blog and my family absolutely loves it. A bit more challenging to make gluten-free, but after about 3 attempts I hit success. Perfectly moist and slightly sweet! Picky hubby and kiddies approved!

1½ cups brown rice flour

1 cup sorghum flour

¼ cup tapioca starch

½ tsp. ground nutmeg

1 tsp. ground cinnamon

1 tsp. salt

1 tsp. xanthan gum

½ tsp. baking soda

1 Tbsp. powdered stevia or 8 packets

3 eggs

2 cups applesauce

½ cup butter, melted

⅓ cup water

¼ tsp. vanilla liquid stevia

2 tsp. vanilla extract

6 cups peeled and sliced apples, divided

juice of ½ lemon

1 Tbsp. ground cinnamon

1 Tbsp. powdered stevia

optional: Sweetened Condensed Milk (p. 127)

1. Preheat oven to 350 degrees. Grease and flour a Bundt pan or 9-inch round cake pan.

2. Whisk first 9 dry ingredients together in a bowl. Set aside. In a stand mixer blend eggs, applesauce, butter, water, vanilla stevia, and vanilla extract until combined well. Set aside.

3. Place apple slices in a large bowl and pour lemon juice over slices. Stir to coat. In a small bowl, whisk together cinnamon and powdered stevia and stir into apple slices to coat. Set aside.

4. With the stand mixer on low speed, gradually pour dry ingredients into wet ingredients in the mixer until incorporated. By hand, pour 4 cups prepared apple slices into batter and stir well.

5. Pour batter into the pan and top with remaining 2 cups prepared apple slices. Bake 1 hour 15 minutes or until a toothpick or skewer in the center comes out clean. Allow to cool 15 minutes. Then loosen edges with a butter knife. Remove from pan to finish cooling on a wire rack. Drizzle warmed homemade Sweetened Condensed Milk over slices if desired.

makes 12 servings

nutritional information

Calories: 241 ◆ Fat: 9.6 g ◆ Sat. Fat: 5.1 g ◆ Cholesterol: 65 mg ◆ Sodium: 312 mg ◆ Carbs: 36.1 g ◆ Fiber: 3.7 g ◆ Sugars: 7.7 g ◆ Protein: 4.6 g

blueberry vanilla dairy-free chia pudding

Another very popular recipe on my blog is dairy-free vanilla chia pudding. This recipe is pretty much based on that same recipe, but with the addition of Blueberry Refrigerator Jam (p. 8). By adding that jam into this, no other sweetener is needed. This is so good it could take on any of those fruit-filled store-bought yogurts!

1 cup unsweetened vanilla almond milk

¼ cup chia seeds

½ cup Blueberry Refrigerator Jam (p. 8)

1. Mix all ingredients and pour into serving glasses. Refrigerate for 10 minutes to set.

makes 2 servings

nutritional information

Calories: 122 ◆ Fat: 7.9 g ◆ Sat. Fat: .6 g ◆ Cholesterol: 0 mg ◆ Sodium: 91 mg ◆ Carbs: 13.4 g ◆ Fiber: 8.2 g ◆ Sugars: 3.3 g ◆ Protein: 7.7 g

gluten-free pie crust 🥧

I've used this pie crust for savory quiche recipes as well as dessert recipes. It's buttery and perfectly flaky. Whenever I make this for guests, no one realizes it's sugar- or gluten-free and often can't believe it when I tell them it is!

1 cup brown rice flour (white rice flour can also be used)

⅓ cup potato flour

⅓ cup tapioca starch/flour

½ tsp. xanthan gum

2 tsp. powdered stevia*

½ tsp. salt

8 Tbsp. cold butter, cut into pieces

1 egg, beaten

3 Tbsp. ice water

*To make this pie crust savory, remove powdered stevia.

1. In a food processor pulse, dry ingredients until combined. Add butter and pulse until formed into crumbs. Add egg and water and pulse until dough comes together.

2. Flour parchment paper. Flour dough a little and roll out to a large circle. Invert pie plate onto dough and then flip dough and pie plate right side up. Shape dough to pie plate, cutting off excess dough on the edges. Cover crust with plastic wrap to chill overnight if not using immediately. Otherwise, continue on with recipe.

3. Prick with fork before baking. When ready to bake, preheat oven to 350 degrees. Place aluminum foil onto dough and add enough dried beans on top of the foil to cover crust bottom. Bake 10 minutes and remove beans. Bake another 10 minutes and cool. Add pie filling as desired. Double crust nutritional information if served with a quiche recipe (makes 6 servings).

makes 12 servings for a dessert pie

nutritional information

Calories: 149 ◆ Fat: 8.4 g ◆ Sat. Fat: 4 g ◆ Cholesterol: 35 mg ◆ Sodium: 158 mg ◆ Carbs: 17.8 g ◆ Fiber: .8 g ◆ Sugars: 0 g ◆ Protein: 1.6 g

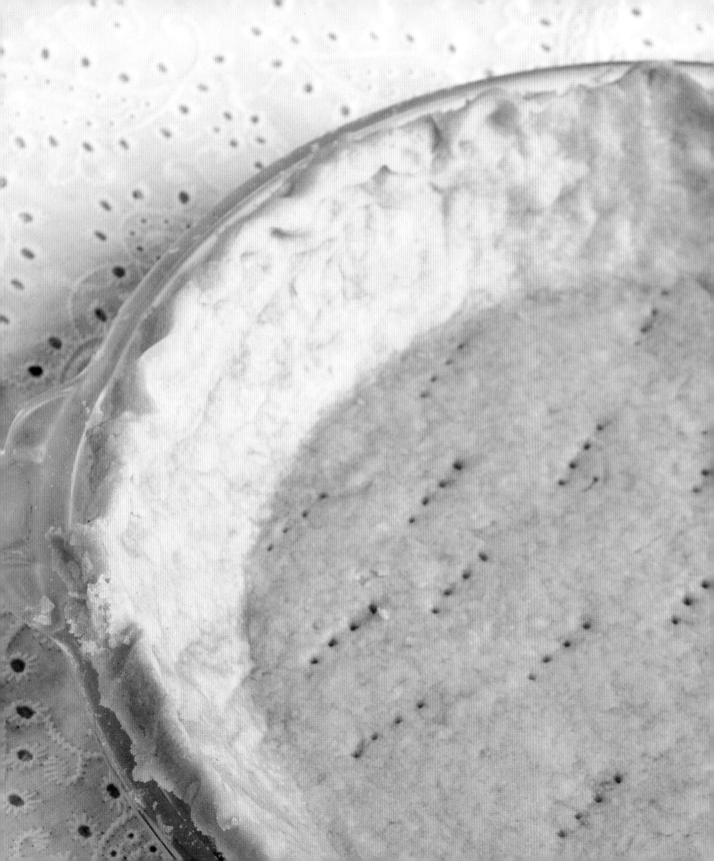

churn-free vanilla ice cream

Once I made the recipe for the homemade Sweetened Condensed Milk (p. 127), I knew a fabulous ice cream had to be made, especially one without the need of an ice cream machine. I'm a vanilla girl by nature, but you could easily adapt this to be chocolate flavored by adding some unsweetened cocoa powder and chocolate stevia. The sugars you see listed in the nutritional information are natural sugars from the milk and cream used.

1¾ cups homemade Sweetened Condensed Milk (p. 127) (14 oz.)

2 tsp. vanilla extract

2 tsp. vanilla liquid stevia

1 Tbsp. vodka

2 cups heavy cream

1. In a bowl stir condensed milk, vanilla, stevia, and vodka and set aside. Beat heavy cream in a stand mixer until stiff peaks form.

2. With a rubber spatula, fold whipped cream into condensed milk mixture. Pour into a 4½ × 8½ loaf pan. Freeze until firm, about 6 hours. Keep frozen up to 1 week.

makes approximately 6 cups @ ½ cup per serving

nutritional information

Calories: 139 ◆ Fat: 8.9 g ◆ Sat. Fat: 5.6 g ◆ Cholesterol: 35 mg ◆ Sodium: 85 mg ◆ Carbs: 7.8 g ◆ Fiber: 0 g ◆ Sugars: 6.8 g ◆ Protein: 5.7 g

shamrock shake 🐮

Oh the infamous shamrock shake that pops up in every commercial in March leading up to Saint Patrick's Day. McDonald's is known for their green ice cream shamrock shake, so of course I had to make a version my kids could enjoy. They won't even taste the spinach, I promise you. My kids never even noticed! You could exchange the milk for half-and-half or light cream to make it creamier, but that will increase the nutritional information here. The sugars you see are from natural sugars in the homemade vanilla ice cream and in the milk used here. There are no added sugars in either the ice cream or this recipe.

2 cups Churn-Free Vanilla Ice Cream (p. 171)

½ cup milk, 1%

½ cup spinach (or use green food coloring)

½ tsp. peppermint extract

optional: a few drops peppermint liquid stevia

1. Let ice cream soften on the counter until it can be scooped and then blend it with remaining ingredients. Taste before adding any stevia.

makes 2 servings

nutritional information

Calories: 308 ♦ Fat: 18.7 g ♦ Sat. Fat: 11.5 g ♦ Cholesterol: 73 mg ♦ Sodium: 207 mg ♦ Carbs: 19 g ♦ Fiber: .2 g ♦ Sugars: 16.9 g ♦ Protein: 13.5 g

graham crackers   *(sub with vegan butter)*

I worked this recipe many times using different combinations of flours before I found the mix that I liked the best and that provided the best resemblance to a typical graham cracker. In order to get that nice brown color I did use some molasses, but very little in comparison to the amount of servings this recipe yields.

⅓ cup butter

¼ cup molasses

1 Tbsp. powdered stevia

¾ cup oat flour

1¼ cups brown rice flour

1 tsp. xanthan gum

2 tsp. ground cinnamon

¼ tsp. ground nutmeg

½ tsp. salt

1. Melt butter and molasses together in the microwave or over low heat on the stove. Whisk stevia, flours, xanthan, cinnamon, nutmeg, and salt together. Pour wet ingredients into dry.

2. Place dough on a Silpat- or parchment-lined baking sheet. Roll dough onto baking sheet. Score cracker squares with a pizza cutter and fork holes to resemble graham crackers. Bake 8–10 minutes or until golden brown. Cool slightly and then break into crackers.

makes 28 crackers @ 2 crackers per serving

nutritional information

Calories: 113 ◆ Fat: 5.1 g ◆ Sat. Fat: 2.3 g ◆ Cholesterol: 12 mg ◆ Sodium: 117 mg ◆ Carbs: 15 g ◆ Fiber: 1.2 g ◆ Sugars: 0 g ◆ Protein: 2 g

homemade marshmallows

I always thought making homemade marshmallows would be such a chore. I waited a long time before even attempting to make one sugar-free. I played around with the recipe, using less and less honey to still get the typical spongy texture of a marshmallow. I'm really pleased with the results. I think we made these half a dozen times before they were perfected. If you want to use all honey you can eliminate the erythritol and powdered stevia and use ¼ cup more honey in the place of those. Still, with the ¼ cup honey used, I'm happy with the reduced sugar in these, and that my kids actually prefer homemade marshmallows!

2 Tbsp. plus ½ tsp. gelatin

1 cup water, divided

½ cup erythritol

2 Tbsp. powdered stevia

¼ tsp. salt

¼ cup honey

2 tsp. vanilla extract

½ tsp. vanilla liquid stevia

1. Lightly dust a 9 × 13 baking dish with powdered erythritol. Set aside.

2. In a stand mixer dissolve gelatin in ½ cup water. Set aside. In a saucepan, whisk remaining ½ cup water with erythritol, powdered stevia, and salt. Then add honey and stir well. Over medium heat, stirring frequently, heat mixture to 245 degrees. Slowly pour water/honey mixture over water/gelatin mixture in the stand mixer.

3. Attach the whipping attachment and beat on high 4–5 minutes or until thick. Pour in vanilla extract and vanilla stevia and beat for 30 seconds more. Immediately spread into the baking dish. Allow to sit at room temperature for 2 hours and then cut into 16 squares.

makes 16 servings

nutritional information

Calories: 19 ◆ Fat: 0 g ◆ Sat. Fat: 0 g ◆ Cholesterol: 0 mg ◆ Sodium: 38 mg ◆ Carbs: 4.3 g ◆ Fiber: 0 g ◆ Sugars: 4.3 g ◆ Protein: .8 g

super food chocolate bar

There's nothing wrong with wanting some chocolate now and then. Often, though, packaged chocolate bars are full of extra ingredients I don't want to ingest. You can find some healthier, sugar-free versions at a health food store, but it often comes with a hefty price tag. This super food idea came while I was browsing chocolate bars at Whole Foods one day. I decided to make a copycat version. It's got a great crunch to it! If you don't like crunch in your chocolate bars just eliminate the first 5 ingredients and you will have a fantastic dark chocolate bar. Use these chocolate bars, Homemade Marshmallows (p. 176), and Graham Crackers (p. 175) to make amazing homemade s'mores like the one shown on page 177.

1 Tbsp. quinoa

1 Tbsp. coconut oil

2 tsp. flaxseeds

2 tsp. chia seeds

2 tsp. sunflower seeds

4 oz. unsweetened baking chocolate

3 Tbsp. coconut oil

¼ tsp. salt

1 tsp. vanilla extract

2 Tbsp. powdered stevia

2 Tbsp. unsweetened almond milk

1. In a small pot with a cover, add quinoa and coconut oil over low heat. Cover and cook until you hear popping sounds and quinoa turns golden brown. Set aside to cool.

2. In a food processor, add flaxseeds, chia seeds, and sunflower seeds. Process until fine. Set aside. Melt chocolate, oil, salt, vanilla extract, stevia, and milk in a saucepan over low heat, stirring frequently until completely smooth and combined. Add seeds and quinoa and stir to coat. Spread into a candy bar mold and refrigerate until hardened, about 1 hour.

makes 2 candy bars @ ¼ candy bar per serving

nutritional information

Calories: 153 ◆ Fat: 15.8 g ◆ Sat. Fat: 10.8 g ◆ Cholesterol: 0 mg ◆ Sodium: 79 mg ◆ Carbohydrates: 6.2 g ◆ Fiber: 3.3 g ◆ Sugars: .2 g ◆ Protein: 2.7 g

chocolate banana peanut butter ice cream with homemade magic shell

This fake-out ice cream became a favorite of mine and the kiddies' as soon as we discovered how much the texture of frozen bananas resemble the texture of ice cream! No sweeteners are needed since the ripe bananas are sweet enough. Adding the peanut butter throws it over the top and you really can't tell it's not ice cream. Perfect to curb that chocolate craving anytime!

2 frozen bananas

2 Tbsp. peanut butter, no sugar added

2 Tbsp. unsweetened cocoa powder

4 Tbsp. Homemade Magic Shell

1. Thaw frozen bananas to a semi-frozen state, and add all ingredients to a food processor. Blend until incorporated. Freeze mixture for 15 minutes for soft serve texture. Top with Homemade Magic Shell!

makes 2 servings

nutritional information

Calories: 210 ♦ Fat: 8.3 g ♦ Sat. Fat: 1.1 g ♦ Cholesterol: 0 mg ♦ Sodium: 61 mg ♦ Carbs: 33.4 g ♦ Fiber: 6.1 g ♦ Sugars: 15.9 g ♦ Protein: 5.8 g

homemade magic shell

When I first made the discovery that coconut oil hardened upon contact with cold foods, I knew the infamous Magic Shell had to be made sugar-free. My kids love it and so do I. You can use this over frozen yogurt, even regular yogurt, or over fruit, like strawberries, for a chocolaty topping. I would suggest using chocolate liquid stevia, but any sweetener you like will work, just add a small amount and then adjust. I felt like a rock star mom when making this for the first time for my kids, their wide eyes staring, jaws dropping, and hysterical shrieks of joy as the chocolate hardened immediately in front of them. You can now be a rock star mom too!

½ cup unsweetened cocoa powder

4 Tbsp. coconut oil, melted

1-4 tsp. liquid stevia

1. Mix all ingredients together, starting with only 1 teaspoon stevia and then adjusting for taste. Stir until smooth. Does not need refrigeration.

makes 8 servings @ 2 Tbsp. per serving

nutritional information

Calories: 72 ♦ Fat: 7.7 g ♦ Sat. Fat: 6.4 g ♦ Cholesterol: 0 mg ♦ Sodium: 1 mg ♦ Carbs: 2.9 g ♦ Fiber: 1.8 g ♦ Sugars: .1 g ♦ Protein: 1.1 g

mom's cheesecake 🍋 🌰

I've made a couple of cheesecakes for the blog, but none that compare to this version. I adapted a recipe of my mom's that is incredible. The combination of sour cream with cream cheese creates height and light texture like no other. Rich, but not too heavy, light but decadent. When my mom tried it she truly could not believe it was gluten- and sugar-free. Coming from my Italian mother, that is a huge compliment.

1½ cups crushed homemade Graham Crackers (p. 175)

⅓ cup butter, melted

3 eggs, room temperature

1 yolk, room temperature

2 tsp. lemon juice

zest of 1 lemon

2 tsp. vanilla extract

2 tsp. vanilla liquid stevia

1 tsp. pure stevia extract or 3 Tbsp. powdered stevia

1 cup sour cream, room temperature

3 (8-oz.) pkgs. light cream cheese, room temperature

1. Preheat oven to 325 degrees. In a food processor, blend graham cracker crumbs with melted butter.

2. Press crumbs into the bottom of a greased springform pan. Set aside. In a stand mixer whisk eggs, yolk, lemon juice, zest, vanilla extract, liquid stevia, and pure stevia extract. Once blended, add sour cream and softened cream cheese, and mix until completely incorporated.

3. Pour into springform pan and place pan in a 9 × 13 baking dish. Pour hot water into baking dish until it reaches half way up the sides of the springform pan. Bake in the center of the oven for 1 hour. Turn off the heat and let cake sit in the oven for another hour. Remove from oven, cover with foil, and chill 4 hours or overnight.

makes 16 slices

nutritional information

Calories: 225 ◆ Fat: 16 g ◆ Sat. Fat: 9 g ◆ Cholesterol: 91 mg ◆ Sodium: 341 mg ◆ Carbs: 12.7 g ◆ Fiber: .7 g ◆ Sugars: 3.3 g ◆ Protein: 7.4 g

chocolate-coated salted chickpeas

Having two boys with nut allergies causes a mother to create a way to help them not feel left out. I'm sure you all know about chocolate-covered peanuts right? Well that is exactly what I was thinking of when I made these for my boys. A little crunch like a nut, but nut-free and chocolate coated.

1 cup Crispy Baked Chickpeas

4 oz. sugar-free chocolate, melted (about ½ cup)

1 tsp. coarse sea salt

1. Toss cooled crispy chickpeas with melted chocolate. Remove covered chickpeas with a fork and lay on a plate to set. Sprinkle with coarse sea salt.

makes 4 servings @ ¼ cup per serving

nutritional information

Calories: 200 ♦ Fat: 10.4 g ♦ Sat. Fat: 6.3 g ♦ Cholesterol: 2 mg ♦ Sodium: 872 mg ♦ Carbs: 29.9 g ♦ Fiber: 6.7 g ♦ Sugars: 0 mg ♦ Protein: 5.9 g

crispy baked chickpeas

This is the basic recipe from my original Garlic Parmesan Roasted Chickpeas (p. 69), but I removed the garlic and parmesan to make these chocolate coated instead. The kids have always loved the Garlic Parmesan Roasted Chickpeas, but they went crazy for these chocolate coated ones!

2 (15.5-oz.) cans chickpeas, rinsed and drained

2 Tbsp. coconut oil, melted, divided

½ tsp. salt

1. Lay drained chickpeas on a paper towel to dry for 30 minutes. Preheat oven to 400 degrees.

2. In a bowl toss 1 tablespoon coconut oil with chickpeas. Add salt and stir to coat.

3. On a baking sheet or Silpat, spread chickpeas out, not overlapping. Drizzle remaining melted coconut oil over chickpeas. Bake for 20 minutes and then stir. Continue to bake and stir up to an hour or until crispy. Nutritional information is for chickpeas without chocolate.

makes 16 servings @ ¼ cup per serving

nutritional information

Calories: 86 ♦ Fat: 2.4 g ♦ Sat. Fat: 1.6 g ♦ Cholesterol: 0 mg ♦ Sodium: 252 mg ♦ Carbs: 13.6 g ♦ Fiber: 2.6 g ♦ Sugars: 0 mg ♦ Protein: 3 g

chocolate cream-filled pumpkin cupcakes with vanilla cream cheese frosting

Tackling a really good cupcake that even the kids will love, and that's not only moist and delicious but also gluten-free and sugar-free, was labor intensive to say the least. I have used pumpkin in recipes with chocolate on my blog, like my whole wheat chocolate pumpkin bread, and I based this cupcake on that recipe. Even if you're not a pumpkin lover, there's only a slight pumpkin flavor here. For the most part, you won't taste anything more than a deep chocolate flavor with a fabulous texture. Don't forgo that frosting in the center. Once made, these will resemble Hostess Cupcakes, and for a sugar-free and gluten-free dessert, I couldn't be happier with them.

1 (15-oz.) can pure pumpkin

½ cup egg whites or 2 eggs

2 eggs

½ cup unsweetened applesauce

½ cup coconut oil

2 oz. unsweetened baking chocolate

1 tsp. vanilla extract

1 tsp. pure stevia extract

2 cups gluten-free flour

½ cup unsweetened cocoa powder

½ tsp. salt

2 tsp. baking powder

1 tsp. baking soda

2 tsp. allspice

2 tsp. pumpkin pie spice

1 tsp. xanthan gum

1 Tbsp. powdered stevia

optional: ½ cup chocolate chips

1. Preheat oven to 350 degrees. Whisk pumpkin, egg whites, eggs, and applesauce together in a bowl. Set aside. Melt coconut oil, chocolate, vanilla, and pure stevia extract in a saucepan over low heat or in a microwavable bowl in 30-second intervals until melted.

2. Whisk flour, cocoa, salt, baking powder, baking soda, spices, xanthan, and powdered stevia together in another bowl. Slowly pour dry ingredients into pumpkin/egg mixture, mixing until combined. Then add melted chocolate mixture and stir to incorporate completely. Stir in optional chocolate chips if using.

3. Pour batter into 12-capacity greased muffin tin or use silicone muffin cups. Bake 30 minutes or until toothpick in center comes out clean. Allow to cool 5 minutes and then remove from pan, loosening edges with a butter knife if needed, and finish cooling on a wire rack.

4. Once completely cool, use an apple corer to remove some center of cupcakes. Be careful not to core through bottom of cupcakes. Make frosting and use a pastry bag or tool to fill center of each cupcake and to top each. Top with shaved chocolate if desired. Nutritional information includes frosting.

makes 12 cream-filled cupcakes

nutritional information

Calories per serving: 303 ♦ Fat: 22.1 g ♦ Sat. Fat: 15.7 g ♦ Cholesterol: 55 mg ♦ Sodium: 400 mg ♦ Carbs: 23.5 g ♦ Fiber: 5.7 g ♦ Sugars: 2.6 g ♦ Protein: 8.2 g

vanilla cream cheese frosting

¼ cup butter, softened

8 oz. cream cheese, light, softened

1 tsp. vanilla extract

½ tsp. vanilla liquid stevia

¼ cup heavy cream

1. Blend butter, cream cheese, vanilla, and stevia until smooth. Pour in heavy cream and blend until combined well.

makes 1¼ cups

single-serve mocha ice cream

Sometimes moms just need their own treat, and since mocha is my favorite, I made a single serve so I honestly didn't have to share with my kids. Not kidding. If you don't like coffee flavor, just substitute the coffee for unsweetened almond milk and you'll have plain chocolate ice cream! It does have a lot of fat, but I don't worry about that as much as the sugar and carbs. Plus, fat makes you feel satisfied and satiated. You could use almond milk or coconut milk as well in place of the heavy cream.

½ cup heavy cream

½ cup brewed, chilled coffee

3 Tbsp. unsweetened cocoa powder

pinch salt

1-2 full droppers chocolate liquid stevia

optional: 1 Tbsp. cacao nibs

1. Add all ingredients into a blender to incorporate, excluding the cacao nibs for now. Taste and adjust sweetener before adding mixture to your ice cream machine.

2. Follow manufacturer's instructions. Mine was perfect in 15 minutes. At the last minute add the cacao nibs if desired. Serve immediately.

makes 1 serving

nutritional information

Calories: 238 ◆ Fat: 23.6 g ◆ Sat. Fat: 13.8 g ◆ Cholesterol: 82 mg ◆ Sodium: 24 mg ◆ Carbs: 11 g ◆ Fiber: 6 g ◆ Sugars: .1 g ◆ Protein: 2.8 g

chocolate sandwich shortbread cookies

These little cookie sandwiches have the best texture and really could compete with any store-bought cookie sandwich. Friends and family rave about them, and they are easy to make!

½ cup butter, unsalted, softened

⅓ cup erythritol

1¼ cups gluten-free flour

½ tsp. salt

¼ tsp. xanthan gum

1 tsp. vanilla extract

¼ tsp. vanilla liquid stevia

½ cup sugar-free chocolate chips

1 Tbsp. coconut oil

1. Preheat oven to 300 degrees. Line a baking sheet with parchment paper. In a stand mixer blend butter with erythritol. Then add flour, salt, xanthan, vanilla extract, and stevia. Mix until dough forms a ball.

2. Roll out onto a floured surface. Cut out shapes if desired. Transfer to baking sheet and bake 20 minutes or until golden. Allow to cool completely before adding chocolate.

3. Melt chocolate chips and coconut oil in a double boiler and then spread ½ teaspoon melted chocolate onto 1 cookie. Place second cookie of same shape on top and set on a wire rack until chocolate hardens. Store in an airtight container.

makes 72 single cookies or 36 chocolate sandwiches @ 2 sandwiches per serving

nutritional information

Calories: 52 ◆ Fat: 4 g ◆ Sat. Fat: 2.6 g ◆ Cholesterol: 7 mg ◆ Sodium: 33 mg ◆ Carbs: 4.9 g ◆ Fiber: .9 g ◆ Sugars: .1 g ◆ Protein: .7 g

chocolate fudge cake

I cannot even begin to tell you how many times I needed to make this recipe before it was perfect. I don't make cakes often but knew a birthday-type cake had to be in this cookbook. What a challenge it created, but I'm thrilled at how it turned out. Gluten- and sugar-free never tasted so good!

6 eggs, room temperature

1 cup applesauce

½ cup butter, melted

¼ cup milk, 1%, room temperature

1 tsp. vanilla extract

1 tsp. vanilla liquid stevia

½ cup erythritol or 2 Tbsp. powdered stevia

⅓ cup coconut flour

¾ cup brown rice flour

⅓ cup unsweetened cocoa powder

1 tsp. baking soda

1 tsp. xanthan gum

1 tsp. baking powder

½ tsp. salt

½ cup sugar-free chocolate chips, melted

Chocolate Fudge Frosting

1. Grease two 8-inch round cake pans, place parchment paper on the bottom of each round cake pan, and then grease the paper or spray the paper with nonstick cooking spray. Preheat oven to 350 degrees.

2. Beat first 6 ingredients together in a stand mixer. Whisk dry ingredients together in a separate bowl. Slowly mix dry ingredients into wet ingredients. Pour melted chocolate chips into mixture and incorporate. Pour batter evenly into each cake pan. Bake 30 minutes or until a skewer in center of cake comes out clean.

3. Cool for 10 minutes. Then invert cakes onto a wire rack to finish cooling, removing the pans. Turn back over and place on a cake plate to frost top of one cake. Place second cake over first frosted cake and frost stacked cakes entirely. Nutritional information for one slice includes frosting.

makes 12 servings

nutritional information

Calories: 266 ♦ Fat: 20.6 g ♦ Sat. Fat: 11 g ♦ Cholesterol: 120 mg ♦ Sodium: 191 mg ♦ Carbs: 20.3 g ♦ Fiber: 5.1 g ♦ Sugars: 1.1 g ♦ Protein: 6.8 g

chocolate fudge frosting

What would a birthday cake or cupcake be without a chocolate fudge frosting? A muffin, I guess. This chocolate fudge frosting is rich, thick, and perfect to top on any dessert. Some stevia brands may be sweeter than others. It depends on how it is processed. Start with less stevia and then add and adjust. If you use erythritol, try to find a brand that is like a powdered sugar texture rather than a granular one, otherwise your frosting might seem gritty.

4 oz. unsweetened baking chocolate

½ cup butter

2 Tbsp. unsweetened cocoa powder

2 Tbsp. powdered stevia or ¼ cup erythritol

pinch salt

⅔ cup heavy cream

2 tsp. pure vanilla extract

2 tsp. liquid stevia

1. In a saucepan over low heat, melt chocolate and butter and stir till smooth. Turn off heat and whisk in cocoa powder, powdered stevia, and salt until blended. Let cool.

2. Whip cream, vanilla, and liquid stevia until peaks form. Slowly blend cooled chocolate mixture into whipped cream. Makes 1¾–2 cups of frosting. Keep refrigerated.

makes 16 servings @ 2 Tbsp. per serving

nutritional information

Calories: 105 ♦ Fat: 11.4 g ♦ Sat. Fat: 6.4 g ♦ Cholesterol: 22 mg ♦ Sodium: 45 mg ♦ Carbs: 2.7 g ♦ Fiber: 1.4 g ♦ Sugars: .1 g ♦ Protein: 1.2 g

lemon bars   *(sub with vegan butter)*

Lemon bars are a traditional favorite for all. I've made these with a few variations, but the final result is one I'm super happy with. Not too much crust and a good creamy filling. You can make this entirely with stevia if you prefer, forgoing the erythritol in the crust and increasing the liquid stevia to a teaspoon. You can also add 2 tablespoons of stevia to the filling to substitute out the erythritol used there. My hubby and children love these bars as they are.

crust

1 cup gluten-free flour

¼ cup erythritol

¼ tsp. xanthan gum

½ tsp. salt

½ tsp. vanilla liquid stevia

6 Tbsp. butter, melted

filling

4 eggs

2 egg yolks

zest and juice of 2 washed and dried lemons, (about ¼ cup each)

¼ cup erythritol

1 tsp. lemon liquid stevia

¼ cup arrowroot powder

2 Tbsp. butter, softened

1. Preheat oven to 350 degrees. Line an 8 × 8 baking dish with 2 sheets of parchment paper with ends that hang over the edges of the pan. To make crust, add all crust ingredients into a food processor and process until dough forms.

2. Spread out dough with fingers onto parchment paper and prick holes into crust with a fork. Bake for 15–20 minutes or until golden brown. Let cool.

3. In a bowl, whisk together eggs and yolks. Add remaining filling ingredients and whisk until combined well. Pour filling over crust and bake 30–35 minutes or until filling is set. Cool to room temperature and refrigerate for 4 hours or overnight.

makes 16 servings

nutritional information

Calories: 109 ♦ Fat: 7.6 g ♦ Sat. Fat: 3.3 g ♦ Cholesterol: 86 g ♦ Sodium: 166 g ♦ Carbs: 7.8 g ♦ Fiber: .9 g ♦ Sugars: .3 g ♦ Protein: 2.8 g

acknowledgments

This book would never have been completed without the helping hands of family and friends to whom I am forever grateful and thankful.

To my love, Jim, my biggest cheerleader. I couldn't imagine my life without you in it, my dear. You have been my constant supporter during this adventure: tackling the dishes that seemed endless and the laundry piling up, whipping up dinner when I just couldn't, ignoring the dirty house and the grouchy wife, never complaining, and always making sure I got to the gym to burn off the stress. My mom always told me, "You know how much someone loves you when they stay by your side even at your worst." You have seen my worst and yet still look at me with those beautiful sea-blue eyes full of love and affection; it surely must be a God thing.

To my children, Joshua, Rebekah, and Jack, the toughest, pickiest food critics I've ever met. You make me strive for the better. You've taught me to never quit; even when I might have failed at a recipe 5 times, your voices echo in my mind to try again. Thank you to Joshua for always telling me I look way younger than any other mother my age, to Rebekah for always being my shopping buddy, and to Jack who tells me every day I'm the most beautiful momma in the world. Everything I do is for you, my precious blessings!

To my mom. You have always shown me what true sacrifice is. That no matter what comes my way, family comes first above all else. That what we leave behind is not the job we had, the times we traveled, or the people we've met, but the memories we've shared with those we love. Pictures and videos are nice, but the written word is truly what speaks to our hearts and souls, which carries on to the next generation. My passion for writing is only because of the amazing example you've given me.

To my dad. You've never had to express how important exercise is because you've shown me by example. Quitting smoking when I was a kid, taking up running, completing 3 marathons, and even at 67, running a half marathon with the boys. It's true that actions speak louder than words, and yours have spoken a thousand!

To Vanessa. Thank you for driving my children to and fro with music classes each week for months so I could work on this cookbook, never complaining and always cheering me with an encouraging word to get to the finish line.

To Laurie, my childhood friend since we were 5. Thank you for your uplifting and thoughtful emails, texts, and cards that always came at just the right time. As the only one I know that still sends handwritten cards by snail mail, I was blessed to be on the receiving end!

To Shawon, my fellow homeschool mother who found her passion in photography. Thank you for coming into my home to shoot photos in my kitchen and make me feel like a celebrity for a day. Your calm demeanor relaxed me and your photos made me look like a movie star. Let's do that again soon!

To my sister-in-law Jane. Thank you for being at my beck and call whenever I cried for help that I just couldn't do it, for going to the market with my list, for cleaning my bathrooms, for chauffeuring the kids to all their activities when I couldn't, and for always being there whenever needed. You have blessed me and the children beyond measure.

To Gina and Joanne. Two wonderful friends who took my kids for play dates countless times so I would have time to cook and write. It's time for a mom's night out, ladies!

To my taste testers and cookbook testers. Thank for you for always being completely honest in reviewing my food and excited to try the next one. For spending your own money and time to make my recipes more than once and for getting your children involved in the kitchen to make my recipes; that has so blessed my heart.

To Andrea, my constant prayer warrior! At just the right time, your call would come and you would pray for me. I can't thank you enough for your friendship and support!

To my brother Ricky, For one day, while digesting from eating a feast at Mom's, suggesting I start a blog and call it Sugar-Free Mom. Knowing I was anything but tech savvy and actually building the blog for me, taking care of all the details I knew nothing about for a good long time until I could pay someone to help. Without you there wouldn't have been a sugarfreemom.com, and I am forever grateful.

To my God and Savior, Jesus Christ, I live and breathe to honor you in all that I do, in all that I say, in all that I share and give. Thank you for turning my misery into a ministry to help others!

To all of *you* readers and fans, I wouldn't be writing this cookbook if it weren't for all of you! Your encouraging comments and emails on my blog as well as Facebook page are what motivate me to keep doing more! I'm so grateful for all of you who try my recipes and come back to share how you liked them. I can't really thank you enough because without you there would never have been a cookbook. I pray you will find these recipes a benefit to your life and family. Thank you for continuing to inspire me!

fan love & testimonies

Corrie says, "I found your blog because a friend of mine told me about one of your recipes, which she pinned on Pinterest. Though I have suspected it for a while, I have recently been diagnosed with hypoglycemia. I have also struggled with my weight over the last several years, along with fatigue and other symptoms of not feeling well. I am just now starting to consider the idea of becoming completely sugar-free. My mother-in-law has been cutting sugar for a while now and many of her recipes seem a bit tasteless. Finding your blog gives me hope that I may just be able to change my eating. In so many ways I work to glorify God, but I am realizing that I am not glorifying him in the foods that I eat. Thank you for sharing your journey and your recipes with others."

Louise says, "I gave up sugar/white flour for over a year and then Christmas happened. I caved and ate . . . and ate . . . and ate sugar and have not been able to get back to sugar-free, clean eating. I have been frustrated and feeling sick, achy, and tired all the time. I have been praying that God would help me find my way back to sugar-free and I stumbled upon your website via Pinterest. I almost cried when I read your story. I knew God brought me here. Thank you for sharing your testimony along with those delicious-sounding recipes!! God's blessing to you and your family."

Domonique says, "'Brain Fog' is totally what I am experiencing today! I am so thankful my search for sugar-free recipes led me to your blog. I'm a true believer that the food we put into our bodies affects our mood and well-being. I think I'm finally ready to commit to the white sugar–free lifestyle and glad I have your blog to offer me great recipe ideas. All the best!!"

Melanie L. says, "Thank you for your testimony. I decided, just a few days ago, because I was feeling so terrible, that I was going to cut out all sugar, all wheat products, and all processed food for a minimum of 30 days to see if it wouldn't help my 'temple of the Holy Spirit' to function properly. I was amazed at how, within 2 days, I was feeling *so* much better already. Today, googling sugar-free recipes, God brought me to your website. All praise to Him who cares for us and perfects that which concerns us! I pray that He will continue to bless you and your family and others that find your website, which is an answer to prayer! In Christ Jesus's love."

Angela says, "Hi Brenda, I just found your blog. . . . It's wonderful! Your ideas and recipes look great and inspire me to begin with one small change at a time.

Overwhelmed=I won't make any changes.
One small change=A step in the right direction towards my goal.

Thanks for sharing your journey!"

Nancy says, "I *love* your site—I subscribe to your blog and follow you on Facebook to make sure I don't miss anything. Because of you, I have tried quinoa, have printed out and tried many recipes, and have really appreciated all the work you do to lead a sugar-free life."

Iris says, "I stumbled upon your Facebook page/website a few days ago, and I just wanted to drop a line to say I think your site is great. I've only just recently started to cut sugar from my diet and your website has been invaluable. There is so much information out there that it can easily become overwhelming and your site seems to condense all the important stuff. I love that your recipes seem easy (since I'm not much of a cook), and this morning I tried the spinach egg bake, which was so easy and tasty. I look forward to trying more very soon. So, thank you. . . . I'm learning lots and [I'm] hopefully on my way to becoming a healthier, sugar-free mom as well."

"Hellooo! My name is Leslie, I'm 24 years old, and I live in NH. I have a severe yeast allergy, and I keep it under control through diet and lifestyle. So I can't eat *any* type of sweetener other than xylitol and stevia. I just stumbled across your website through Pinterest and I already have oatmeal in the crock pot for breakfast tomorrow. I'm so excited!! So, I just wanna say that I loooove your recipes and your website, and I think what you're doing is fan-stinkin-tastic! :) Especially for people like myself, who have such a restricted diet, it's people like *your*self that help us to keep our sanity. So thanks! And keep up the awesome work!"

Crystal says, "I just wanted to say that I am so grateful I came upon your website! A friend of mine has Pinterest and had pinned your recipe for Baked Oatmeal to Go muffin cups [Personal-Sized Baked Oatmeal Cups]. I am so excited to try them this weekend and wanted to know more about you, so I clicked on your 'about me' and was so encouraged to hear your story as well as your faith in Jesus Christ. I too am a believer in our sweet Lord Jesus and have a similar story with finding and maintaining a healthy weight. Thank you again for the creation of your site and sharing of your story!"

Rebecca says, "My husband and I are working for the Department of State and are currently in Thailand. Since two years I have been now on the 'losing weight the right way trip' and so far lost 40 pounds. During my journey I discovered several things. I am hypersensitive to sugar and single carbohydrates. So one day I was searching for a recipe and it brought up your page. I just want to say thank you very much for all your work. I like to cook from scratch because for me that is easier and when you are always in a different country you will not get all your products you are used to. Yours was one of the few websites that I found with food from scratch. I still have to order a few things online (certain flours and chia seeds) but you help me a lot. So I just wanted to drop you a note and tell you thanks. And in a way you are supporting our troops" (Rebecca is at the American Embassy in Bangkok).

Julianna says, "I have never written a blogger before! As a stay-at-home mom, I am a huge fan of 'mom blogs' and spend my free time browsing these sites for innovative ways to provide for my family. I stumbled upon your blog a couple of weeks ago after I took the plunge to embark on a low glycemic/sugar-free/white flour–free lifestyle. Your page has been the biggest blessing to me that I simply had to personally write you to thank you. When I turned my back on the processed nasties (sugar, white flour, and so on), I did so with a bold determination to create a healthier life for my family but thought I was giving up good taste and variety. Since I didn't grow up eating this way, my frame of reference was narrow, and I had a limited understanding of the vast opportunity of foods still available to me. Your blog has broadened my horizons, and I am so thrilled that I don't have to choose between good health and good taste. I have spent so much time drooling over your recipes and trying out new things that I can't wait to share with my family and friends. I am happy to say that because of the effort you have put forth, I know this can be a lifelong journey of healthy eating for my family, and not just our current 'diet.' So I am overwhelmed with gratitude and want you to know how very much your time and effort are appreciated."

Cooking Measurement Equivalents

Cups	Tablespoons	Fluid Ounces
⅛ cup	2 Tbsp.	1 fl. oz.
¼ cup	4 Tbsp.	2 fl. oz.
⅓ cup	5 Tbsp. + 1 tsp.	
½ cup	8 Tbsp.	4 fl. oz.
⅔ cup	10 Tbsp. + 2 tsp.	
¾ cup	12 Tbsp.	6 fl. oz.
1 cup	16 Tbsp.	8 fl. oz.

Cups	Fluid Ounces	Pints/Quarts/Gallons
1 cup	8 fl. oz.	½ pint
2 cups	16 fl. oz.	1 pint = ½ quart
3 cups	24 fl. oz.	1½ pints
4 cups	32 fl. oz.	2 pints = 1 quart
8 cups	64 fl. oz.	2 quarts = ½ gallon
16 cups	128 fl. oz.	4 quarts = 1 gallon

Other Helpful Equivalents

1 Tbsp.	3 tsp.
8 oz.	½ lb.
16 oz.	1 lb.

Metric Measurement Equivalents

Approximate Weight Equivalents

Ounces	Pounds	Grams
4 oz.	¼ lb.	113 g
5 oz.		142 g
6 oz.		170 g
8 oz.	½ lb.	227 g
9 oz.		255 g
12 oz.	¾ lb.	340 g
16 oz.	1 lb.	454 g

Approximate Volume Equivalents

Cups	US Fluid Ounces	Milliliters
⅛ cup	1 fl. oz.	30 mL
¼ cup	2 fl. oz.	59 mL
½ cup	4 fl. oz.	118 mL
¾ cup	6 fl. oz.	177 mL
1 cup	8 fl. oz.	237 mL

Other Helpful Equivalents

½ tsp.	2½ mL	
1 tsp.	5 mL	
1 Tbsp.	15 mL	

index

g

garlic parmesan roasted chickpeas, 69
gluten-free pie crust, 168
graham crackers, 175
grain-free chocolate glazed donuts, 9
gram's butter balls, 153
greek veggie burgers, 111

h

healthier fried rice, 51
homemade magic shell, 180
homemade marshmallows, 176
homemade powdered sugar substitute, 150

i

italian sausage & pepper quesadillas, 41
italian spinach meatloaf muffins, 104

l

lemon bars, 195
lemon pudding cakes, 158
lemonade, 141
lightened-up crock pot chicken herb stroganoff, 94

m

mayo-free chicken salad lettuce wraps, 38
mayo-free cilantro lime dip, 89
mayo-free creamy coleslaw, 80
mayo-free ranch dressing, 118
mayo-free tartar sauce, 122
mediterranean chicken cutlets, 79
mini bacon chicken cheddar quinoa bites, 43
mini italian stuffed meatballs with quick marinara sauce, 108
mini zucchini cheese bites, 59
mocha protein coffee frappe, 139
mock tater tots, 54
mom's cheesecake, 183

n

no-bake nut-free granola bars, 20
nut-free florentine lace cookies, 150
nut-free magic bars, 160
nut-free tart shell, 156

o

oat flour pizza dough, 92
oatmeal breakfast cookies, 34
oatmeal seed bread, 6

about the author

Brenda Bennett's passion for cooking began at the age of 5, kneeling on a chair by her grandmother's side and helping her roll homemade gnocchi on a flour-covered butcher-block table.

Her love affair with cooking was a mere hobby while she taught as a special educator and earned a master's degree in education. After the birth of her second child, however, she had to give up sugar. With sheer determination and a deep desire to still enjoy chocolate, her love affair with food embarked on a new journey: learning to develop recipes free of refined sugars and flours.

After discovering peanut, tree nut, and soy allergies in 2 of her 3 children, making homemade healthier versions of the treats they loved became a necessity. She transitioned to the position of homeschooling mom of 3, recipe developer, food writer, photographer, and blogger. She focuses on making wholesome, delicious food, free of processed flours and sugars, to feed her family, and she shares with friends and fans on www.sugarfreemom.com. She lives in Rhode Island with her husband, 3 children, and their dog, Ruby. When she isn't cooking, blogging, or writing, she can be found at spin class, camping, volunteering in Cub Scouts, or in the position of transportation engineer shuttling her children to karate, dance, Boy Scouts, soccer, or softball.

Shawon Davis Photography

0 26575 14498 7